... ... GN
C... ...IZE
WITHOUT FORFEITING PROTEIN

That's a strange mouthful, but it's far more memorable than a list of *ei* words that are the exception to the "*i* before *e*" rule. Whatever your personal spelling demon, there's a mnemonic device to defeat it.

Try out some of these tricks of the trade on frequently misspelled (*Miss Pell* can't *misspell*) words:

How do you remember the "n" in Wednesday?
Pronounce it Wed Nes Day.
Strawberry shortcake is my favorite dessert.
I'll love you tr*uly* in J*uly*

There's no *x* in *ecstasy*.
But there is pure delight in

DEMONIC
MNEMONICS

Demonic Mnemonics

Demonic Mnemonics

800 Spelling Tricks
for 800 Tricky Words

MURRAY SUID

A LAUREL BOOK
Published by
Dell Publishing
a division of
Bantam Doubleday Dell Publishing Group, Inc.
666 Fifth Avenue
New York, New York 10103

This book is for Ron Harris

Illustrator: Jim M'Guinness

ISBN: 0-440-20647-2

Reprinted by arrangement with Fearon Teacher Aids

Printed in the United States of America
Published simultaneously in Canada

July 1990

10 9 8 7 6 5 4 3 2 1
OPM

Introduction

The Problem

English spelling is weird (or is it *wierd*?). For almost every rule-abiding word—*mat, cat, sat*—there's a demon whose spelling makes little or no sense.

Some demons have silent letters: **sign, herb, knee**. Others seem to be missing letters: *welcome* (instead of *wellcome*).

There are demon pairs—words that sound alike but have different spellings—*pain* and *pane, Mary* and *marry*. Other pairs are pronounced differently but spelled confusingly alike—*dessert* and *desert, hoped* and *hopped*.

What about suffix pairs like **-ance** and **-ence**? They mean the same thing. They're pronounced alike. But there's no rule to tell which suffix to use with a particular word. The same is true for **-able** and **-ible**.

The Solution

Conventional wisdom recommends drilling such demons into submission. Unfortunately, most people can list dozens of words they've studied and looked up again and again, yet they're still not sure of the correct spelling.

A more powerful way to defeat a demon word is to confront it with a *mnemonic* (nĭ–'mahn–ick) device. A mnemonic is a memory trick. It works by creating an association or link between the demon word and an easy-to-spell word or phrase. You may know some mnemonics already. A few are classics:

> The school princi**pal** is your **pal**. The princi**ple** that serves as a guideline is a ru**le**.

> A stationary, unmoving object st**a**nds still. The station**e**ry that you write letters on is pap**er**.

Mnemonics are sometimes silly, farfetched, or downright outrageous. So much the better, as long as they do their job—to help you master words that are equally outrageous and irrational in the ways they are spelled.

This Book

Demonic Mnemonics offers memory tricks for more than 800 of the most commonly misspelled words. Entries were chosen from a dozen lists of demon words and also from the suggestions of teachers, writers, and editors.

Each entry has three parts. The first part is the *definition*. Knowing what the word means is especially important when dealing with homonyms (*capital* and *capitol*) or other frequently confused pairs (*desert* and *dessert*). Rather than formal, dictionary-type definitions, informal definitions are given so that each word is readily identifiable.

Next comes the *trouble spot*. Boldface type highlights the letter or letters that cause the spelling problem. Awareness of the tricky part of the word strengthens the mnemonic link. When the boldface type alone isn't enough to explain the problem, a parenthetical comment provides clarification.

The third part is the *trick*, the mnemonic device intended to find a permanent niche in your memory, so you'll never misspell that demon again.

Sample Entry

fundamental: basic
trouble spot: fund**a**mental
trick: Saying **"amen"** is fund**amen**tal.

In some instances, one of the rules found at the back of this book relates to the tricky spelling of demon words (see pages 163–174). When that is the case, the rule is noted.

Sample Entry

bookkeeper: one who keeps track of business transactions
trouble spot: boo**kk**eeper
trick: (Compounders, pages 165–166)

Certain mnemonics are immediately memorable. Many mnemonics don't stick quickly, however, and you may have to look up a mnemonic two or three times before you finally get it. But it's worth the effort. Memorizing a mnemonic is almost always easier than trying to memorize a word whose spelling will continue to elude you.

The Eight Basic Links
As you use *Demonic Mnemonics* you will discover that there are eight basic kinds of links.
1. *The built-in-word link.* Many eccentric

words contain easy-to-spell clue words. The mnemonic sentence simply links the demon word to its inner clue word.

You h**ear** with your **ear**.

Forty soldiers stormed the **fort**.

2. *The definitional link.* The meaning of a word can sometimes provide the clue to correct spelling. In such cases, the mnemonic takes the form of a definition.

A b**each** is land by the s**ea**.

A b**eech** is a tr**ee**.

3. *The analogous pattern link.* This kind of link usually works best to remind you whether a demon is in fact one word or two.

We will go **all together** or **all separately**.

4. *The story sentence link.* This kind of mnemonic tells a story. Some mnemonics combine several recalcitrant words, all irregular in the same way. By turning the words into a story, you link them together and have an easier time remembering each one.

N**ei**ther l**ei**sured for**ei**gn counterf**ei**ter could s**ei**ze **ei**ther w**ei**rd h**ei**ght without forf**ei**ting prot**ei**n.

That's a strange mouthful, but it's far more memorable than a list of **ei** words that are the exception to the *"I* before *E"* rule.

Another kind of story link states the problem itself in a memorable way:

Use both **i**'s (eyes) in sk**ii**ng.

5. *The acronym link.* A sentence is invented based on each letter of the demon word. Take *arithmetic:*

Arithmetic: A rat **i**n **t**he **h**ouse **m**ight **e**at **t**he **i**ce **c**ream.

Strange but true, many people find mastering this 11-word sentence a fun way to remember that arithmetic has an **e** in it—between the **m** and the **t**.

6. *The pronunciation link.* You can learn how to spell some words by inventing memorable ways of pronouncing—or mispronouncing—them:

Pronounce *Wednesday* "Wed–nes–day."

Naturally, this kind of exaggerated pronounciation should be used only in private. But note that widespread usage will often transform the pronunciation of a word to conform to its spelling. Many people pronounce the **t** in *often*, and *Webster's New Collegiate Dictionary* now gives that pronunciation legitimate standing.

7. *The etymological link.* This kind of link uses one form of a word to clarify the spelling of another. For example, because it is silent, the **c** in *muscle* sometimes is forgotten, so a helpful mnemonic links *muscle* to the word *muscular* in which the **c** is pronounced.

If you have **musc**les, you're **musc**ular.

8. *The descriptive link.* This kind of mnemonic simply describes the problem in a succinct, memorable way.

There's no **x** in **ecstasy**.

Warning!
Demonic Mnemonics is not meant to be read from cover to cover. If spelling drill tests your patience, trying to drill 800 mnemonics into your head will test your sanity—doubly so because many of the mnemonics don't make any conventional sense. The sense they do make is speller's sense.

For best results treat each mnemonic as strong medicine of the last resort. Use mnemonics only with those words that have resisted more conventional attack—careful reading, application of the rules (see pages 163–174), and mild drill.

Inventing Your Own Mnemonics
There are two reasons why you might wish to create your own memory tricks. First, a mnemonic found in this book may simply not work for you. Mnemonics, after all, are more quirky than scientific.

Second, if you're like most people, you will be stumped by some words that everyone else finds simple. Don't be embarrassed. Just invent your own personal demon-slayer. (The author did just that when, after ten years, he still couldn't remember if his mother-in-law spelled her name *Jenny* or *Jennie*. Finally, he linked the woman's maiden name—*Fine*—to her first name—Jenn**ie**.)

Creating mnemonics takes a bit of brain work, but it's fun. Even intermediate-level children can play the game once they're shown how. (At the dinner table a fifth-grader came up with this mnemonic for remembering where all the l's go in *parallel:* First a pair of l's, then one l.) Mnemonic-making is a good exercise for creative thinking.

The secret to creating mnemonics is being familiar with the eight basic linking patterns. In the beginning, keep them handy, as you would a recipe. If you can't forge one kind of association, try another. Go right down the list until something clicks for you.

You'll also want a good dictionary close by. The etymology and definitions found in an entry often provide the basic material for a mnemonic.

Two working assumptions may prove useful as well.

1. *Anything goes.* Don't shy away from silly or sensational associations. You may even dis-

agree with what your trick sentence says. Suppose you write, "Bu**sin**ess is a **sin**." Perhaps you like business. Possibly you own 10,000 shares of IBM. Yet, if "Bu**sin**ess is a **sin**" works for you, don't reject it.

2. *More than anything goes.* There can be—and there usually are—many spelling tricks for taming a single demon. Even if at first you succeed, you might want to keep trying. You may come up with another trick that works even better.

absence: being away
trouble spot: absen**c**e
trick: When you **c**ut a **c**lass, that's an absen**c**e.

absolutely: completely
trouble spot: absolut**e**ly
trick: I abso**lute**ly love **lute** music.

absorption: soaking up
   trouble spot: absor**p**tion
   trick: When you so**p** something **up**,
   that's absor**p**tion.

abundance: great supply
   trouble spot: abun**d**ance
   trick: Food was in abun**dance** at the
   dance.

accelerate: increase speed
   trouble spot: a**cc**elerate
   trick: To a**cc**elerate the **c**able **c**ar, pull
   this lever.

accident: unexpected happening
   trouble spot: a**cc**i**dent**
   trick: The **c**able **c**ar a**cc**i**dent** made a
   dent.

accidentally: happening by chance
   trouble spot: a**cc**iden**tally**
   trick: The **c**able **c**ar a**cc**iden**tally** ran
   over **Sally**.

accommodations: lodgings
   trouble spot: a**cc**o**mm**odations
   trick: The a**cc**o**mm**odations were so
   small that you could measure them in
   cc's (cubic centimeters) or **mm**'s
   (millimeters).

account: calculation
    trouble spot: a**cc**ount
    trick: An a**cc**ount is a **c**al**c**ulation.

accumulate: collect
    trouble spot: a**cc**umulate (one **m**)
    trick: A**cc**umulate **c**ho**c**olate **c**hips, not **m**oney.

accurate: exact
    trouble spot: a**cc**urate
    trick: Are **c**u**c**koo **c**lo**c**ks a**cc**urate?

accuse: find at fault
    trouble spot: a**cc**use
    trick: I a**cc**use you of eating my **c**ho**c**olate **c**hips.

accustomed: in the habit of
    trouble spot: a**cc**ustomed
    trick: **T**om is a**cc**us**t**omed to **c**able **c**ars.

ache: dull pain
    trouble spot: a**ch**e
    trick: I have **a ch**est a**ch**e.

achievement: accomplishment
    trouble spot: a**chieve**ment
    trick: I was so shy that saying "**Hi, Eve**" was a big a**chieve**ment.

Did you see the queen's acquaintance at the dance?

acknowledgment: recognition
    trouble spot: acknowle**dgm**ent (also
    acknowledgement)
    trick: The dictionary makes this
    acknowle**d**gment: an **e** or not.

acquaintance: someone known, not a friend
    trouble spot: a**c**qu**a**int**a**nce
    trick: Did you **c** (see) the **qu**een's
    a**c**qu**a**int**ance** at the d**a**nce?

acquitted: found innocent
    trouble spot: a**c**qui**tt**ed
    trick: I **c** (see) you were a**c**qui**tt**ed of
    stealing the **k**i**tt**y.

acre: measure of land
    trouble spot: ac**re**
    trick: This **acre** is s**acre**d.

across: from one side to the other
    trouble spot: **across**
    trick: We took **a cross across** the street.

ad: advertisement
    trouble spot: **ad** (one **d**; not *add*)
    trick: This **ad** makes me m**ad**.

additional: extra
    trouble spot: **add**itional
    trick: I need an **add**itional **Dad**dy.

address: place where one lives or gets mail
    trouble spot: **add**ress
    trick: **Add** my name to your **add**ress book.

adhesive: sticky substance
    trouble spot: adhe**s**ive
    trick: An adhe**s**ive is **s**ticky.

adjust: adapt
    trouble spot: a**d**just
    trick: When you a**d**just, you a**d**apt.

advantageous: favorable
    trouble spot: advantageous
    trick: **Age** is advant**age**ous.

advertise: make known
  trouble spot: advert**ise**
  trick: It's w**ise** to advert**ise**.

advice: counsel
  trouble spot: adv**ice** (not *advise*)
  trick: I need adv**ice** about driving on
  ice.

advisable: wise
  trouble spot: advi**s**able (no **e** between **s**
  and **a**)
  trick: Wearing **sable** is advi**s**able in
  winter.

advise: give advice
  trouble spot: Advi**se** (not *advice*)
  trick: Be w**ise** when you advi**se**.

affect: influence
  trouble spot: **a**ffect (not *effect*)
  trick: **A**nimals can **a**ffect me.

against: opposed to
  trouble spot: ag**ai**nst
  trick: It's hard to **gain** ag**ain**st the wind.

aggravate: make worse or annoy
  trouble spot: a**g**gra**v**ate
  trick: **G**ood grief! **Ava** a**g**gra**v**ates me.

aide: assistant
>   trouble spot: aid**e** (silent **e**; not *aid*)
>   trick: An a**ide** is on your s**ide**.

aisle: passageway
>   trouble spot: **ais**le (not *isle*)
>   trick: **Rais**e the **ais**le.

alcohol: intoxicating liquid
>   trouble spot: al**co**hol
>   trick: My **coho**rt drinks al**coho**l.

allegiance: loyalty
>   trouble spot: **all**e**gi**ance
>   trick: **All** pledge **allegia**nce to the **gia**nt.

alley: narrow street
>   trouble spot: all**ey**
>   trick: Keep your **ey**es on the all**ey**.

allotted: granted
>   trouble spot: **all**o**tt**ed
>   trick: **All** the b**ott**led water was **allott**ed.

allowance: money given regularly
>   trouble spot: **all**o**w**ance
>   trick: I need **all** my **all**o**w**ance for the d**a**nce.

All pledge allegiance to the giant.

all ready: completely prepared
   trouble spot: **all ready** (two words; not *already*)
   trick: If you're **all ready**, you can **all read**.

all together: as a single group
   trouble spot: **all together** (two words; not *altogether*)
   trick: We will go **all together** or **all separately**.

almost: nearly
   trouble spot: almost (one **l**)
   trick: I **alm**ost gave **Al** some **alm**s.

a lot: a great deal
> trouble spot: **a lot** (two words; not *alot*)
> trick: You can spend **a little** or **a lot**.

already: earlier
> trouble spot: already (one word; not *all ready*)
> trick: Did **Al al**ready leave?

altar: table for sacred purposes
> trouble spot: alt**ar** (not *alter*)
> trick: An al**ta**r is a kind of **ta**ble.

alter: change
> trouble spot: alt**er** (not *altar*)
> trick: Alt**er** the t**er**ms of the contract.

altogether: completely
> trouble spot: altogether (one **l**; not *all together*)
> trick: The **alto** sings **alto**gether flat.

always: at all times
> trouble spot: always (one **l**)
> trick: **Al al**ways wins.

amateur: nonprofessional
> trouble spot: amat**eur**
> trick: Oh, what **a mate u** (you) **r** (are), you **amateur**.

ambitious: eager
   trouble spot: ambitious
   trick: I'm not a **bit** am**bit**ious.

amendment: addition
   trouble spot: amendment (one **m**)
   trick: An a**mend**ment **mend**s the law.

amiable: friendly
   trouble spot: am**i**able
   trick: **Am I able** to be **ami**able?

amount: quantity
   trouble spot: a**m**ount (one **m**)
   trick: The **amount** was less than **a mount**ain.

analyze: separate into parts
   trouble spot: anal**yze**
   trick: **Y** (why) anal**yze ze**bras?

angel: supernatural being
   trouble spot: an**gel** (not *angle*)
   trick: **Angel**s are **angel**ic.

angle: shape made when two straight lines
      meet
   trouble spot: an**gle** (not *angel*)
   trick: The **gl**ider came in at a sharp
   an**gle**.

Ann wrote the announcement in cement.

annihilate: destroy completely
trouble spot: a**nn**ihila**t**e (one **l**)
trick: If you say **"Hi" late** to **Ann** she
will **annihilate** you.

announcement: notice
trouble spot: a**nn**ou**n**ce**ment**
trick: **Ann** wrote the **ann**ou**n**ce**ment** in
cement.

annual: yearly
trouble spot: a**nn**ual
trick: Invite **Ann** to our **ann**ual picnic.

answer: reply
trouble spot: answer
trick: Pronounce *answer* "ans–wer."

antidote: remedy
    trouble spot: ant**i**dote
    trick: I h**id** the ant**id**ote.

anxiety: worry
    trouble spot: an**x**iety
    trick: **X** out anxiety.

apologize: express regret
    trouble spot: apo**l**ogize (one **l**)
    trick: A **polo** player shouldn't a**pologize** for lack of s**ize**.

apparatus: instruments or equipment
    trouble spot: **app**arat**us**
    trick: Does this **app**arat**us** make **us** h**app**y?

apparently: evidently
    trouble spot: **app**ar**e**ntly
    trick: You're **app**ar**e**ntly h**app**y about the low **rent**.

appearance: act of appearing; how a person or thing seems
    trouble spot: a**pp**earance
    trick: The band was h**app**y to make an **app**ea**rance** at the d**ance**.

appointment: engagement
    trouble spot: a**pp**ointment
    trick: This is a h**app**y a**pp**ointment.

appreciate: think well of
trouble spot: a**pp**reciate
trick: I a**pp**reciate being ha**pp**y.

appropriate: fitting
trouble spot: a**pp**ropri**ate**
trick: The a**pp**le I **ate** was a**pp**ropri**ate**.

approval: favorable opinion
trouble spot: a**pp**roval
trick: Your a**pp**roval makes me ha**pp**y.

apricot: kind of fruit
trouble spot: a**p**ricot (one **p**)
trick: Are a**p**ri**c**ots ripe in A**p**ri**l**?

architect: designer of buildings
trouble spot: ar**ch**itect
trick: The ar**ch**itect designed the ar**ch**.

arctic: near the North Pole
trouble spot: ar**c**tic
trick: The ar**c**tic is **c**old.

argument: disagreement
trouble spot: arg**um**ent (no **e** between **u** and **m**)
trick: An arg**um**ent **gum**s up the works.

arithmetic: science of computing real numbers
trouble spot: arith**m**etic
trick: **Arithmetic: A r**at **i**n **t**he **h**ouse **m**ight **e**at **t**he **i**ce **c**ream.

ascend: go up
trouble spot: a**sc**end
trick: A**sc**end this **sc**ary hill.

ascertain: make sure
trouble spot: a**sc**ertain
trick: When you **ascertain** a fact, be **as certain** as you possibly can.

asinine: silly
trouble spot: a**s**inine (one **s**)
trick: Is it **a sin** to be **asin**ine?

assassin: killer of an important person
trouble spot: a**ss**a**ss**in
trick: An **assass**in is a double **ass**.

assistant: helper
trouble spot: a**ss**is**t**ant
trick: An **ass** and an **ant** are my **ass**is**t**ants.

asterisk: starlike mark (*)
trouble spot: asteri**sk**
trick: Is there a **risk** in using an aste**risk**?

athlete: person active in a sport
trouble spot: at**hl**ete (no **e** between **h** and **l**)
trick: After her b**ath let** the **athlet**e rest.

An ass and an ant are my assistants.

attacked: assaulted
   trouble spot: atta**c**ked (no **t**)
   trick: When they att**acked**, we b**acked**
   away.

attendance: presence
   trouble spot: att**e**n**d**ance
   trick: **At ten** we'll take **attendance** for
   the **dance**.

attention: notice
   trouble spot: attention
   trick: Pay **atten**tion **at ten**.

attitude: state of mind
    trouble spot: at**t**itude
    trick: **Batt**le your bad at**t**itude.

attorney: lawyer
    trouble spot: attorn**eys**
    trick: The attorn**eys** have lost their k**eys**.

Australia: continent in the South Pacific
    trouble spot: Aust**ra**lia (no **i** between **a** and **l**)
    trick: **Al** is from cen**tral** Aust**ra**lia.

autumn: fall
    trouble spot: autum**n** (silent **n**)
    trick: **N**ovember is the end of autum**n**.

auxiliary: assisting
    trouble spot: auxi**li**ary
    trick: There's a **liar** in the auxi**liar**y group.

awful: terrible
    trouble spot: awfu**l** (one **l**)
    trick: **Ul**cers are awf**ul**.

axle: shaft on which a wheel turns
    trouble spot: ax**le**
    trick: They're having an ax**le** sa**le**.

B

baboon: monkey
   trouble spot: ba**b**oon (one **b**)
   trick: A **bab**oon is like a **bab**y.

bachelor: unmarried man
   trouble spot: ba**c**helor (no **t** between **a**
   and **c**)
   trick: **Bach** was not a **bach**elor.

baggage: luggage
   trouble spot: ba**gg**age
   trick: **G**et a **g**ood **g**rip on your ba**gg**age.

balance: bring to equilibrium
   trouble spot: ba**l**ance (one **l**)
   trick: It's hard to b**alance a lance.**

balloon: inflatable rubber bag
   trouble spot: ba**ll**oon
   trick: A **ball**oon is a **ball**.

ballots: papers that register votes
   trouble spot: ba**ll**ots
   trick: **Ball**ots will be counted at the
   ball.

banana: kind of fruit
   trouble spot: ba**na**na
   trick: It's a **no-no** to **ban a na**ked
   banana.

barbecue: party where food is cooked over
         an open fire
   trouble spot: barb**e**cue
   trick: Summer's our **cue** to hold a
   barb**ecue**.

bare: without covering
   trouble spot: b**are** (not *bear*)
   trick: Do you c**are** if I'm b**are**?

bargain: good buy, agreement
   trouble spot: barg**ai**n
   trick: What did you **gain** in that
   bar**gain**?

basically: fundamentally
   trouble spot: basic**ally**
   trick: Basic**ally**, I trust our **ally**.

basis: foundation
>trouble spot: basis (one **s**)
>trick: **Sis** learned the ba**sis** of mathematics.

bazaar: market
>trouble spot: b**azaar** (not *bizarre*)
>trick: Our market is called the Triple A (**aaa**) Bazaar.

bear: large mammal
>trouble spot: b**ear** (not *bare*)
>trick: Did you ever **eat** b**ear** m**eat**?

beautiful: very pretty
>trouble spot: b**eautiful**
>trick: **Beautiful: B**oys **e**at **a**pples **u**nder **t**rees **i**n **f**all **u**nder **l**eaves.

beggar: person who asks for charity
>trouble spot: beg**gar**
>trick: The beg**gar** came from **far** away.

beginning: start
>trouble spot: begi**nn**ing
>trick: At the beg**inn**ing we stayed at the **inn**.

behavior: actions
>trouble spot: beha**vio**r
>trick: Watch out for **vio**lent beha**vio**r.

Our neighbor's eight beige reindeer weighed
too much to send by freight.

beige: grayish tan
>trouble spot: b**ei**ge
>trick: Our n**ei**ghbor's **ei**ght b**ei**ge
>r**ei**ndeer w**ei**ghed too much to send by
>fr**ei**ght.

believable: credible
>trouble spot: belie**va**ble (no **e** between **v**
>and **a**)
>trick: **Eva** is not belie**va**ble.

believe: accept as true
>trouble spot: bel**ie**ve
>trick: Never bel**ie**ve a **lie**.

benefited: got an advantage
trouble spot: bene**f**ited (one **t**)
trick: My **bite** bene**fite**d from braces.

berserk: state of violent rage
trouble spot: be**r**serk
trick: I went **ber**serk in **Ber**lin.

bicycle: two-wheeled vehicle
trouble spot: bi**c**ycle
trick: Don't ride your bi**cy**cle in **icy** weather.

binoculars: optical device
trouble spot: bi**n**oculars (one **n**)
trick: The **bin**oculars are in the **bin**.

bizarre: odd
trouble spot: bi**z**arre (not *bazaar*)
trick: It was another **bizarre** show **biz arre**st.

blizzard: violent storm
trouble spot: bli**zz**ard
trick: You won't find a bu**zz**ard bu**zz**ing in a bli**zz**ard.

bookkeeper: one who keeps track of business
              transactions
trouble spot: boo**kk**eeper
trick: (Compounders, pages 165–166)

bought: purchased
> trouble spot: b**ough**t
> trick: I th**ough**t I'd b**ough**t en**ough**
> c**ough** syrup to make it thr**ough** this
> r**ough**, t**ough** winter.

boulevard: wide street
> trouble spot: b**ou**levard
> trick: This **bou**levard is **ou**t of **bou**nds.

boundary: edge
> trouble spot: bound**ary**
> trick: M**ary**'s lamb crossed the
> bound**ary** of the school g**ar**den.

brake: device for slowing or stopping a vehicle
> trouble spot: br**ake** (not *break*)
> trick: For heaven's s**ake**, use the br**ake**!

breadth: width
> trouble spot: brea**d**th (not *breath*)
> trick: The **bread** has **bread**th.

break: cause to come apart
> trouble spot: br**ea**k (not *brake*)
> trick: **Break bread** with me.

breathe: take air into the lungs and then let it
out
> trouble spot: breath**e** (not *breath*)
> trick: Breath**e** with **e**ase.

brilliant: outstanding
   trouble spot: bri**ll**iant
   trick: The Three Stooges were bri**ll**iant
   with si**ll**iness.

bruise: injure
   trouble spot: br**ui**se
   trick: A br**ui**se can r**ui**n fr**ui**t.

budget: plan for matching income to outgo
   trouble spot: bu**dg**et
   trick: **Bud**, don't **budge** from your
   budget.

built: constructed
   trouble spot: b**ui**lt
   trick: Have you any g**ui**lt about what **u**
   (you) and **I** b**ui**lt?

buoy: floating objcct
   trouble spot: b**uo**y (not *boy*)
   trick: A b**uo**y warns of **u**nderwater
   objects.

burglar: thief
   trouble spot: burg**lar**
   trick: A burg**lar** commits **lar**ceny.

business: a company
   trouble spot: bu**si**ness
   trick: Bu**si**ness is a **sin**.

buzzard: kind of bird
    trouble spot: bu**zz**ard
    trick: You won't find a bu**zz**ard bu**zz**ing in a bli**zz**ard.

C

cafeteria: self-service restaurant
    trouble spot: ca**fe**teria
    trick: Is it **safe** to eat in the ca**fe**teria?

calendar: chart of the days of the year
    trouble spot: calend**ar**
    trick: The calend**ar** is a list of **da**tes.

callous: lacking pity
    trouble spot: ca**llou**s (not *callus*)
    trick: Don't **call ou**t to a **callou**s person for help.

callus: hardened patch of skin
    trouble spot: ca**llu**s (not *callous*)
    trick: **Call us** if you have a **callus**.

campaign: series of planned actions
  trouble spot: campai**g**n (silent **g**)
  trick: Campai**g**n for clean **g**overnment.

cancel: do away with
  trouble spot: can**c**el
  trick: Can**c**el the **cel**ebration.

candidate: person running for an elective office
  trouble spot: can**di**date
  trick: Was the **candid**ate **candid**?

cannon: large, mounted piece of artillery
  trouble spot: can**n**on (not *canon*)
  trick: **Ann** can**no**t fire the **cann**on.

canoe: narrow, light boat
  trouble spot: can**oe**
  trick: This can**oe** leaks like a sh**oe**.

canvas: closely woven, coarse cloth
  trouble spot: canva**s** (one **s**; not *canvass*)
  trick: The circus was in a **vas**t can**vas** tent.

canvass: survey
  trouble spot: canva**ss** (not *canvas*)
  trick: Let's canv**ass** the m**ass** of people.

This canoe leaks like a shoe.

capacity: amount of room or space inside
    trouble spot: capa**ci**ty
    trick: What is the capa**city** of this **city** for tourists?

capital: uppercase letter
    trouble spot: capit**a**l (not *capitol*)
    trick: **A** is the first capit**a**l letter.

capital: government city
    trouble spot: capit**a**l (not *capitol*)
    trick: There's a lot of **tal**k in the capit**al** city.

capital: money used to run a business
    trouble spot: capit**a**l (not *capitol*)
    trick: **Ca**sh is a form of **ca**pital.

capitol: building where a legislature meets
    trouble spot: capit**o**l (not *capital*)
    trick: The capit**o**l building has a d**o**me.

captain: commanding officer
    trouble spot: capt**ai**n
    trick: The capt**ai**n is the m**ai**n officer.

career: life work
    trouble spot: car**ee**r
    trick: She made a car**ee**r selling b**ee**r.

carrying: taking from one place to another
    trouble spot: carr**y**ing
    trick: (Y-Enders, pages 173–174)

cavalry: troops on horses
    trouble spot: ca**val**ry
    trick: The ca**val**ry soldiers were **val**iant.

cemetery: burial place
    trouble spot: c**e**m**e**t**e**ry
    trick: Life in a c**e**m**e**t**e**ry is all **e**'s (easc).

cereal: breakfast food
    trouble spot: **c**ereal (not *serial*)
    trick: **C**ornflakes **c**ereal is **real** good.

certain: sure
    trouble spot: cert**ai**n
    trick: Is the capt**ai**n cert**ai**n it will r**ai**n?

changeable: not staying the same
trouble spot: chang**ea**ble
trick: You should always be **able** to keep the **change** in **changeable**.

changing: becoming something else
trouble spot: chan**gi**ng (no **e** between **g** and **i**)
trick: When something is **hanging** it can't be **changing**.

chaperon: person who supervises another person or persons
trouble spot: **ch**aperon (also spelled *chaperone*)
trick: My **chap**eron is a good **chap**.

chateau: large country house
trouble spot: chat**eau**
trick: After **tea u** (you) can visit my chat**eau**.

chauffeur: driver of an automobile
trouble spot: chau**ff**eur
trick: Our chau**ff**eur hates the tra**ff**ic in **Eur**ope.

chief: leader
trouble spot: ch**ie**f
trick: **Hi**, ch**i**ef.

chocolate: food made from cocoa beans
  trouble spot: cho**cola**te
  trick: I like **cola** better than cho**cola**te.

choose: select
  trouble spot: ch**oo**se (not *chose*)
  trick: What would a l**oose** g**oose** ch**oose**?

chose: past tense of *choose*
  trouble spot: ch**ose** (not *choose*)
  trick: My n**ose** ch**ose** this r**ose**.

Cincinnati: city in Ohio
  trouble spot: Cin**c**i**nn**ati
  trick: We stayed **in** the **inn** at **Cin**cinnati.

clientele: customers
  trouble spot: clien**tele**
  trick: Our clien**tele** reach us by **tele**phone.

clothes: wearing apparel
  trouble spot: cl**othe**s (not *cloths*)
  trick: Wear your **othe**r cl**othe**s.

college: school of higher learning
  trouble spot: col**le**ge
  trick: If you want to go to co**lle**ge, eat **all** your **vege**tables.

Are you the lone colonel?

colonel: chief officer of a regiment
   trouble spot: co**lonel** (pronounced
   kernel)
   trick: Are you the **lone** colonel?

colossal: huge
   trouble spot: co**loss**al (one **l**)
   trick: This was a co**loss**al **loss**.

coma: unconsciousness
   trouble spot: co**m**a (one **m;** not *comma*)
   trick: Will the patient **com**e out of the
   coma?

comfortable: providing ease
   trouble spot: com**fort**able
   trick: The **fort** has a com**fortable table.**

coming: approaching
    trouble spot: co**m**ing (no **e** between **m** and **i**)
    trick: They're co**m**ing home in a **min**ute.

comma: punctuation mark (,)
    trouble spot: comma (not *coma*)
    trick: **Comm**a errors are **comm**on.

commercial: advertisement
    trouble spot: com**m**ercial
    trick: Here's a co**m**mercial for **M&M**'s®

commission: group of people doing work for the government
    trouble spot: co**mm**i**ss**ion
    trick: A co**mm**i**ss**ion doubles the work—and the letters **mm** and **ss**.

committee: group of people working together
    trouble spot: co**mmittee**
    trick: A co**mmittee** doubles the work—and the letters **mm**, **tt**, and **ee**.

communication: means of sending information
    trouble spot: co**mm**unication
    trick: **M**ass **m**edia are used in co**mm**unication.

community: people living as a group
    trouble spot: co**mm**unity
    trick: We're a su**mm**er co**mm**unity.

comparatively: relatively
    trouble spot: compar**a**tively
    trick: The **rat** is compar**a**tively bright.

comparison: estimation of similarities and
            differences
    trouble spot: compar**i**son
    trick: **Paris** is beyond com**paris**on.

compatible: going together
    trouble spot: compat**i**ble
    trick: Is science compat**ible** with the
    Bible?

compelled: forced
    trouble spot: compe**ll**ed
    trick: I was com**pell**ed to **spell** the word
    correctly.

competent: capable
    trouble spot: comp**e**tent
    trick: **Compete**nt people **compete**.

competition: contest
    trouble spot: comp**e**tition
    trick: I'm entering my **pet** in the
    com**pet**ition.

complacent: smug
   trouble spot: compla**c**ent
   trick: I'm com**place**nt about my **place**
   in life.

complement: something that completes
   trouble spot: compl**e**ment (not
   compliment)
   trick: A **comple**ment **comple**tes.

completely: totally
   trouble spot: comple**te**ly
   trick: **Pete** comple**te**ly did it.

complexion: appearance
   trouble spot: comple**x**ion
   trick: I have a **complex complex**ion.

compliment: expression of approval
   trouble spot: compl**i**ment (not
   complement)
   trick: I l**i**ke compl**i**ments.

compromise: give up something in order to
                  agree
   trouble spot: compromi**se**
   trick: Be w**ise**, compromi**se**.

conceive: imagine
   trouble spot: conc**ei**ve
   trick: **Once I've** done something, I can
   conc**ei**ve of it.

condemn: pass an adverse judgment
trouble spot: condem**n** (silent **n**)
trick: When you condem**n**, you express
condem**n**ation.

confidence: trust
trouble spot: confidence
trick: I have confid**ence** in the f**ence**.

Connecticut: U.S. state
trouble spot: Connecticut
trick: **Connect** with **Connect**icut.

conscience: sense of right and wrong
trouble spot: con**sci**ence
trick: Does **science** have a con**science**?

consensus: agreement
trouble spot: con**sens**us
trick: **Send us** the con**sens**us you have
reached.

consistent: always the same
trouble spot: consis**t**ent
trick: This **tent** gives us consis**tent**
protection.

consul: government official
trouble spot: con**sul** (not *council* or
counsel)
trick: **Consul**t with the **consul**.

contemptible: deserving scorn
    trouble spot: contempt**i**ble
    trick: The **Bi**ble says sin is
    contempt**ible**.

continually: going on without interruption
    trouble spot: continu**all**y
    trick: **Sally** is continu**all**y helping me.

control: restraint
    trouble spot: contro**l** (one **l**)
    trick: Practice self-contro**l**.

controlled: directed
    trouble spot: contro**ll**ed
    trick: The **troll** contro**ll**ed the bridge.

convenience: anything that makes things
               easy
    trouble spot: conven**i**ence
    trick: Sc**i**ence is a conven**ience**.

cooperate: work in harmony
    trouble spot: c**oo**perate
    trick: Hens **coop**erate in the **coop**.

cord: thick string or rope
    trouble spot: **cord** (not *chord*)
    trick: Tie the **cor**k with the **cor**d.

The troll controlled the bridge.

cordial: friendly
   trouble spot: cord**ia**l
   trick: After you **dial**, speak in a cor**dial** voice.

corduroy: heavy cotton fabric
   trouble spot: cord**u**roy
   trick: Cor**dur**oy is **dur**able.

corps: group of workers or soldiers
   trouble spot: cor**ps** (silent **p** and **s**; not *corpse*)
   trick: The cor**ps** has ca**ps**.

corpse: dead body
   trouble spot: corps**e** (not *corps*)
   trick: You'll **e**nd as a corps**e**.

correspondence: communication by letters
trouble spot: correspond**e**nce
trick: I hu**rr**y my correspon**den**ce by writing in my **den**.

corroborate: confirm
trouble spot: co**rr**oborate
trick: Don't w**orr**y, I'll co**rr**oborate your story.

cough: sudden expulsion of air from lungs
trouble spot: c**ough**
trick: I th**ough**t I'd b**ough**t en**ough** c**ough** syrup to make it thr**ough** this r**ough**, t**ough** winter.

council: legislative body
trouble spot: coun**c**il (not *counsel* or *consul*)
trick: The **c**ity coun**c**il is a group of **c**itizens.

counsel: give advice
trouble spot: coun**s**el (not *council* or *consul*)
trick: Coun**sel sel**dom.

counterfeiter: person who makes phony money
> trouble spot: counter**fei**ter
> trick: **Nei**ther **lei**sured for**eig**n counter**fei**ter could s**ei**ze **ei**ther w**ei**rd h**ei**ght without forf**ei**ting prot**ei**n.

courageous: brave
> trouble spot: cour**age**ous
> trick: In this **age**, being cour**age**ous counts.

course: way
> trouble spot: c**our**se (not *coarse*)
> trick: We've lost **our** c**our**se.

courteous: polite
> trouble spot: c**ourt**eous
> trick: Be **court**eous in **court**.

criticism: informed judgment
> trouble spot: criti**ci**sm
> trick: A **critic** writes **critic**ism.

criticize: analyze the worth of a work
> trouble spot: criti**ciz**e
> trick: The **critic** won't **criticize** the p**riz**e.

curiosity: interest
> trouble spot: curi**osi**ty
> trick: Curi**osi**ty doesn't **sit** still.

curriculum: course of studies
  trouble spot: curriculum
  trick: Don't **hurry** through the
  cur**r**iculum.

customer: patron
  trouble spot: custo**m**er
  trick: **Homer** is a good custo**m**er.

cylinder: chamber in an engine
  trouble spot: cyli**n**der
  trick: An i**c**y cy**li**nder will **hinder** an
  engine.

D

deceive: mislead
  trouble spot: dece**i**ve
  trick: (*I* before *E*, pages 169–170)

decent: good
  trouble spot: de**c**ent (not *descent*)
  trick: Re**cent**ly you've been **decent**.

defendant: the accused in a legal case
　　trouble spot: defend**a**nt
　　trick: The defend**ant** was an **ant**.

democracy: a system of government
　　trouble spot: democra**c**y
　　trick: Democ**racy** is **racy**.

dependent: relying on
　　trouble spot: depend**e**nt
　　trick: I'm depend**ent** on you for my
　　r**ent**.

descent: downward slope
　　trouble spot: de**sc**ent (not *decent*)
　　trick: Begin the **sc**ary de**sc**ent.

describe: tell or write about
　　trouble spot: d**e**scribe
　　trick: **De**scribe the **de**sign.

description: picture in words
　　trouble spot: descri**p**tion
　　trick: The **script** gives a detailed
　　de**scrip**tion of the t**rip**.

desert: dry region
　　trouble spot: de**s**ert (one **s**; not *dessert*)
　　trick: The de**s**ert is filled with **s**and.

desert: reward or punishment
> trouble spot: de**s**ert (one **s**; not *dessert*)
> trick: A just **desert** is what you **deser**ve.

desirable: worth wanting
> trouble spot: desir**a**ble (no **e** between **r** and **a**)
> trick: Are **rab**ies desi**rab**le?

despair: hopelessness
> trouble spot: de**s**pair
> trick: I feel **des**pair when I sit at my **des**k.

desperate: hopeless
> trouble spot: desper**ate**
> trick: I **rate** you despe**rate**.

despise: hate
> trouble spot: desp**i**se
> trick: It's not w**ise** to desp**ise**.

dessert: sweet ending of a meal
> trouble spot: de**ss**ert (not *desert*)
> trick: **S**trawberry **s**hortcake is my favorite de**ss**ert.

destroy: ruin
> trouble spot: de**s**troy
> trick: **De**finitely **de**stroy **de**mons.

Definitely destroy demons.

develop: bring to fruition
trouble spot: develo**p** (no **e** at the end)
trick: Devel**op** until you st**op**.

development: outcome of some action
trouble spot: develo**pm**ent (no **e**
between **p** and **m**)
trick: Let's discuss this develo**pm**ent in
the **P.M.**

dictionary: book of words
trouble spot: diction**a**ry
trick: M**ary** reads the diction**ary**.

difference: unlikeness or space between persons or things
trouble spot: di**ff**e**r**ence
trick: What's the **diff**e**r**ence if we **differ**
in the **end**?

difficult: hard to do or understand
    trouble spot: di**ff**icult
    trick: The two **f**'s are doubly di**ff**icult.

dilemma: predicament
    trouble spot: di**l**e**mm**a (one **l**; two **m**'s)
    trick: **L**et's help **Emm**a with her
    di**lemm**a.

dining: eating
    trouble spot: di**n**ing (one **n**)
    trick: This is f**ine** d**in**ing.

disappear: vanish
    trouble spot: di**s**a**pp**ear
    trick: Th**is app**le d**isapp**ears.

disastrous: calamitous
    trouble spot: disa**str**ous (no **e** between **t**
    and **r**)
    trick: The **astro**naut's crash was
    dis**astro**us.

discipline: branch of learning; rules of behav-
          ior
    trouble spot: di**sci**pline
    trick: The di**scip**line of **sci**ence draws
    no **line**s.

discuss: talk over
    trouble spot: discu**ss**
    trick: Don't f**uss**; just disc**uss**.

dissatisfied: not pleased
    trouble spot: di**ss**atisfied
    trick: (Nay-Sayers, pages 171–172)

divided: parted
    trouble spot: di**vi**ded
    trick: My **divi**ng **divi**ded the water.

divine: terrific
    trouble spot: di**vi**ne
    trick: **Divi**ng's **divi**ne.

doctor: a physician
    trouble spot: doct**or**
    trick: Follow the doct**or**'s **or**ders.

does: accomplishes
    trouble spot: d**oes**
    trick: D**oes** she put her t**oes** in her sh**oes**?

doesn't: contraction of *does not*
    trouble spot: does**n't**
    trick: (Contract'ns, pages 166–167)

dominant: controlling
    trouble spot: domin**ant**
    trick: The queen **ant** is domin**ant**.

don't: contraction of *do not*
    trouble spot: do**n't**
    trick: (Contract'ns, pages 166–167)

dormitory: rooms for sleeping
    trouble spot: dor**mit**ory
    trick: I live in the dor**mit**ory at **MIT**.

drunkenness: state of being drunk
    trouble spot: drunke**nn**ess
    trick: (*Ness*-Enders, page 172)

dyeing: process of coloring with dye
    trouble spot: dy**e**ing (not *dying*)
    trick: When **dyeing**, leave the **dye in**.

dying: process of giving up life
    trouble spot: d**y**ing (not *dyeing*)
    trick: When there's d**ying**, there's
cr**ying**.

E

easel: tripod to hold an artist's canvas
    trouble spot: eas**e**l
    trick: This **ease**l goes up with **ease**.

ecstasy: great delight
> trouble spot: **ecs**tasy (no **x**)
> trick: There's no **x** in **ecstasy.**

effect: bring about
> trouble spot: **e**ffect (not *affect*)
> trick: It takes **eff**ort to **eff**ect
> **e**nthusiasm.

eighth: the one after *seventh*
> trouble spot: eigh**th**
> trick: **Eight** + **h** = **eighth.**

either: one or the other of two
> trouble spot: **ei**ther
> trick: N**ei**ther l**ei**sured for**ei**gn
> counterf**ei**ter could s**ei**ze **ei**ther w**ei**rd
> h**ei**ght without forf**ei**ting prot**ei**n.

eligible: qualified
> trouble spot: eli**gi**ble
> trick: Though the rules are ri**gi**d, you're
> eli**gi**ble.

embarrassing: making self-conscious
> trouble spot: emba**rr**a**ss**ing
> trick: It's doubly emba**rr**a**ss**ing to forget
> the double **r** (**rr**) and double **s** (**ss**) in
> emba**rr**a**ss**ing.

Neither leisured foreign counterfeiter could seize either weird height without forfeiting protein.

eminent: famous
  trouble spot: em**i**nent
  trick: **Mine** is the most em**ine**nt family.

emphasize: stress
  trouble spot: empha**size**
  trick: Skyscrapers empha**size size**.

endeavor: task
  trouble spot: end**eavo**r
  trick: A h**eav**y end**eavo**r takes eff**o**rt.

enemy: foe
  trouble spot: **e**ne**m**y
  trick: My **ene**my has **ene**rgy.

engineer: train operator
  trouble spot: engin**ee**r
  trick: An engin**ee**r must s**ee** and st**ee**r.

enormous: huge
   trouble spot: enorm**ou**s
   trick: A th**ou**sand p**ou**nds is an
   enorm**ou**s am**ou**nt.

enough: sufficient
   trouble spot: en**ough**
   trick: I th**ough**t I'd b**ough**t en**ough**
   c**ough** syrup to make it thr**ough** the
   r**ough**, t**ough** winter.

enterprise: venture
   trouble spot: enterpri**s**e
   trick: Chart the **rise** of free enterp**rise**.

envelope: container for a letter
   trouble spot: envelop**e** (not *envelop*)
   trick: Even a d**ope** can seal an
   envel**ope**.

environment: surroundings
   trouble spot: envi**ron**ment
   trick: **Ron** values his envi**ron**ment.

equipment: tools needed for a job
   trouble spot: equi**p**ment (one **p**)
   trick: What equ**ipment** came with this
   sh**ipment**?

equipped: supplied
 trouble spot: equi**pp**ed
 trick: This car was fully equi**pp**ed when
 sh**ipped.**

essential: necessary
 trouble spot: e**ss**ential
 trick: Is this m**ess ess**ential?

evidently: clear, obvious
 trouble spot: eviden**tly** (no **al** between **t**
 and **l**)
 trick: Eviden**tly** the answer will shor**tly**
 appear.

exaggerate: magnify beyond the facts
 trouble spot: exa**gg**erate
 trick: **G**ood **g**rief! How you exaggerate!

exceed: go beyond
 trouble spot: e**x**ceed
 trick: There's no e**x**cuse when you
 exceed the safe sp**eed.**

excellent: first class
 trouble spot: ex**c**ellent
 trick: We have an **exc**ellent **exc**use.

except: other than
 trouble spot: **ex**cept (not *accept*)
 trick: There's no **exc**use **exc**ept illness.

exercise: activity
   trouble spot: e**x**er**c**ise (no **c** between **x** and **e**)
   trick: It's w**ise** to e**x**er**t** yourself when you **exercise**.

exhausted: tired out
   trouble spot: ex**h**austed (silent **h**)
   trick: I was so **exha**usted, I **exha**led noisily.

existence: life
   trouble spot: exist**e**nce
   trick: It went out of exis**ten**ce **ten** years ago.

expense: cost
   trouble spot: expen**s**e
   trick: The **pens** are an extra ex**pens**e.

explanation: reason
   trouble spot: exp**la**nation (contrast with *explain*)
   trick: This **plan** calls for an ex**plan**ation.

extension: going beyond
   trouble spot: exten**s**ion
   trick: Pull the ex**tens**ion cord **tens**e.

extraordinary: unusual
> trouble spot: extr**a**ordinary
> trick: Pronounce *extraordinary* "extra–
> ordinary."

extreme: drastic
> trouble spot: extr**eme**
> trick: We'll have to try an ext**reme**
> **reme**dy.

F

familiar: intimate
> trouble spot: famil**iar**
> trick: A **liar** has to be famil**iar** with the
> facts.

fascinating: intriguing
> trouble spot: fa**sc**inating
> trick: **Sc**ary things can be fa**sc**inating.

February: second month of the year
> trouble spot: Feb**r**uary
> trick: **Br**other, it's cold in Feb**r**uary.

fertile: rich in resources
    trouble spot: fert**ile**
    trick: The N**ile** valley is fert**ile**.

fiend: evil person
    trouble spot: f**ie**nd
    trick: **Fie** on you, f**ie**nd.

fiery: hot
    trouble spot: f**ie**ry
    trick: You can d**ie** in a f**ie**ry crash.

finally: at last
    trouble spot: fin**ally**
    trick: S**ally** fin**ally** came home.

flammable: easily set on fire
    trouble spot: fla**mm**able
    trick: Trees are more fla**mm**able in su**mm**er.

flannel: kind of cloth
    trouble spot: fla**nn**el
    trick: Don't wear fla**nn**el in a tu**nn**el.

flies: moves through the air
    trouble spot: fl**ie**s
    trick: A **lie** fl**ie**s.

forehead: part of the face
    trouble spot: for**e**head
    trick: Your **fore**head goes be**fore**.

Don't wear flannel in a tunnel.

foreign: from another country; unusual
    trouble spot: for**ei**gn
    trick: N**ei**ther l**ei**sured for**ei**gn
count**er**f**ei**ter could s**ei**ze **ei**ther w**ei**rd
h**ei**ght without forf**ei**ting prot**ei**n.

forest: tree-covered land
    trouble spot: fo**r**est (one **r**)
    trick: Where is the **rest** of the fo**rest**?

foreword: preface
    trouble spot: fo**re**word (not *forward*)
    trick: **Word**s be**fore** make a **foreword**.

forfeiting: losing
trouble spot: forf**ei**ting
trick: N**ei**ther l**ei**sured for**ei**gn
counterf**ei**ter could s**ei**ze **ei**ther weird
h**ei**ght without forf**ei**ting prot**ei**n.

forgotten: not remembered
trouble spot: forgo**tt**en
trick: I **got ten** things, but I've
for**gotten** what they are.

forth: onward
trouble spot: f**or**th (not *fourth*)
trick: Go **for**th from the **fort**.

forty: a number
trouble spot: f**or**ty
trick: **Fort**y soldiers stormed the **fort**.

forward: toward the front
trouble spot: f**or**ward (not *foreword*)
trick: All those **for war**, step **forwar**d.

fourth: the one after *third*
trouble spot: f**our**th (not *forth*)
trick: The **four**th number is **four**.

Frances: a girl's name
trouble spot: Franc**es** (not *Francis*)
trick: Franc**es** is h**er** name; Franc**is** is
h**is** name.

Francis: a boy's name
   trouble spot: Francis (not *Frances*)
   trick: Francis is his name; Frances is
   her name.

freight: material transported
   trouble spot: fr**ei**ght
   trick: Our n**ei**ghbor's **ei**ght b**ei**ge
   r**ei**ndeer w**ei**ghed too much to send by
   fr**ei**ght.

friend: a person one knows well and cares
      for
   trouble spot: fri**e**nd
   trick: A fri**e**nd won't li**e**.

fulfill: carry out
   trouble spot: fulf**ill** (also spelled *fulfil*)
   trick: The **el**f w**ill** fulf**ill** your wish.

fundamental: basic
   trouble spot: fund**a**mental
   trick: Saying "**amen**" is fund**amen**tal.

furniture: chairs, tables
   trouble spot: furnit**ure**
   trick: It s**ure** is lovely furnit**ure**.

further: beyond, to a greater degree
   trouble spot: f**ur**ther
   trick: Don't h**ur**t me any f**ur**ther.

G

gallon: measure equal to four quarts
trouble spot: ga**ll**on
trick: **All** we need is a ga**ll**on of gas.

genius: brilliant person
trouble spot: gen**ius** (no **o** between **i** and **u**)
trick: **I** before **us** ends every gen**ius**.

gentleman: gracious man
trouble spot: gent**lem**an
trick: The gent**lem**an ordered a **lem**on.

genuine: authentic
trouble spot: gen**uine**
trick: This w**ine** is gen**uine**.

glimpsed: viewed
trouble spot: glim**ps**ed
trick: I glim**ps**ed the ecli**ps**e before I colla**ps**ed.

gnarled: knotted
    trouble spot: **gn**arled (silent **g**)
    trick: The **gn**arled **gn**ome **gn**ashed his
    teeth as he **gn**awed a **gn**at.

gnashed: ground
    trouble spot: **gn**ashed (silent **g**)
    trick: The **gn**arled **gn**ome **gn**ashed his
    teeth as he **gn**awed a **gn**at.

gnat: tiny two-winged insect
    trouble spot: **gn**at (silent **g**)
    trick: The **gn**arled **gn**ome **gn**ashed his
    teeth as he **gn**awed a **gn**at.

gnawed: cut, bit, and wore away with the
        teeth
    trouble spot: **gn**awed (silent **g**)
    trick: The **gn**arled **gn**ome **gn**ashed his
    teeth as he **gn**awed a **gn**at.

gnome: a dwarf
    trouble spot: **gn**ome (silent **g**)
    trick: The **gn**arled **gn**ome **gn**ashed his
    teeth as he **gn**awed a **gn**at.

government: system for maintaining order in
            a society
    trouble spot: g**overn**ment
    trick: A **govern**ment **govern**s **over** the
    society.

The gnarled gnome gnashed his teeth
as he gnawed a gnat.

governor: chief administrative officer of a
    state government
  trouble spot: gover**nor**
  trick: Neither the senat**or nor** the
  gover**nor** voted.

graham: kind of flour
  trouble spot: gra**ha**m
  trick: I'll have **ham** on my gra**ham**
  cracker.

grammar: rules for how a language works
trouble spot: gra**mm**ar
trick: **Gramma** sure knows her
grammar.

grateful: thankful
trouble spot: gr**ateful** (one **l**)
trick: Be gr**ateful** we don't h**ate** bu**lb**s.

gravel: mixture of pebbles and cement
trouble spot: grav**el**
trick: Put some **grave**l on my **grave**.

grieve: sorrow for
trouble spot: gr**ie**ve
trick: **I** gr**ieve** for **Eve**.

grievous: deplorable
trouble spot: grie**vo**us (no **i** between **v**
and **o**)
trick: It's gr**ievous** to **vou**ch for a
misch**ievous** kid.

grocery: food store
trouble spot: gro**c**ery
trick: I'm using the gro**c**ery **c**art.

guarantee: assure the quality
trouble spot: g**uar**antee
trick: This **guar**antee **guar**ds you for
fr**ee**.

guitar: stringed musical instrument
    trouble spot: g**ui**tar
    trick: I wear a s**ui**t when I play g**ui**tar.

H

handful: small amount
    trouble spot: handfu**l** (one **l**)
    trick: I bought a handf**ul** of b**ul**bs.

handsome: good-looking
    trouble spot: han**d**some
    trick: You have **hands**ome **hands**.

hangar: storage place for an airplane
    trouble spot: hang**ar** (not *hanger*)
    trick: A han**gar** is a **gar**age for planes.

hanger: device for hanging clothes
    trouble spot: hang**er** (not *hangar*)
    trick: I feel **anger** when clothes aren't
    on h**anger**s.

happened: occurred
    trouble spot: ha**pp**ened
    trick: I'm **happ**y it **happ**ened.

harass: bother
    trouble spot: ha**r**ass (one **r**)
    trick: **Ha**, how c**rass** to **harass**!

hardware: equipment
    trouble spot: hard**wa**re
    trick: Military hard**war**e is for **war**.

having: possessing
    trouble spot: ha**vi**ng (no **e** between **v** and **i**)
    trick: You can't have an **e** in **having**.

Hawaii: U.S. state
    trouble spot: Hawa**ii**
    trick: Hawa**ii** is **i**sland after **i**sland.

hazard: danger
    trouble spot: ha**z**ard (one **z**)
    trick: **Zap** the h**azard** in the **yard**.

heaven: dwelling place of God
    trouble spot: h**ea**ven
    trick: When do you l**eave** for h**eave**n?

There were heroes facing torpedoes while eating tomatoes and potatoes.

height: topmost point
    trouble spot: h**ei**ght
    trick: N**ei**ther l**ei**sured for**ei**gn counterf**ei**ter could s**ei**ze **ei**ther w**ei**rd h**ei**ght without forf**ei**ting prot**ei**n.

heroes: plural of hero
    trouble spot: her**oes**
    trick: There were her**oes** facing torped**oes** while eating tomat**oes** and potat**oes**.

hideous: horrible to see
    trouble spot: hid**e**ous
    trick: **Hide** from a **hide**ous monster.

hindrance: obstacle
> trouble spot: hin**dr**ance (no **e** between
> **d** and **r**)
> trick: **Dra**t, all the frag**rance**s at the
> ent**rance** are a hind**rance**.

hippopotamus: large animal
> trouble spot: hippo**potamus**
> trick: Fill the hippo**potamus pot** for **us**.

hoard: hide supplies
> trouble spot: h**oa**rd (not *horde*)
> trick: Don't h**oa**rd the **oa**rs.

hoarse: having a harsh or grating sound
> trouble spot: h**oa**rse (not *horse*)
> trick: I r**oa**red myself h**oa**rse.

holiday: special day
> trouble spot: ho**li**day
> trick: Put a **lid** on ho**li**day celebrating.

hoping: desiring
> trouble spot: ho**pi**ng (no **e** between **p**
> and **i**; not *hopping*)
> trick: I'm ho**pi**ng the **pin** won't stick
> me.

horde: wandering tribe; large, moving crowd
> trouble spot: h**orde** (not *hoard*)
> trick: **Orde**r the h**orde** to move.

hosiery: stockings
    trouble spot: hos**ie**ry
    trick: I like f**ie**ry hos**ie**ry.

hostile: not hospitable
    trouble spot: host**ile**
    trick: The N**ile** River is host**ile**.

Hungary: European country
    trouble spot: Hung**ary** (not *hungry*)
    trick: **Hungar**y is the home of
    Hungarians.

hungry: wanting food
    trouble spot: hun**gr**y (not *Hungary*)
    trick: Your stomach **gr**owls when **y**ou're
    hun**gr**y.

hypocrisy: pretense
    trouble spot: hypoc**ri**sy
    trick: Hypoc**ri**sy is **ri**sky.

ignorant: uninformed
trouble spot: igno**rant**
trick: Igno**rant** people **rant**.

illumination: light
trouble spot: i**ll**umination
trick: Neon **ill**umination makes me **ill**.

imitate: copy
trouble spot: i**m**itate (one m)
trick: **Limit** what you **imit**ate.

immediately: right away
trouble spot: i**mm**edi**ate**ly
trick: We **ate** our **M&M**'s® i**mm**ediately.

immigrant: person who moves into a country
trouble spot: i**mm**igrant
trick: **Imm**igrants came to **M**aine and **M**innesota.

impossible: not possible
>   trouble spot: impo**ss**ible
>   trick: It's impo**ss**ible to mi**ss** with the **B**i**ble**.

incidentally: by the way
>   trouble spot: incident**all**y
>   trick: Incident**all**y, where's **S**a**ll**y?

independent: self-reliant
>   trouble spot: indepen**d**ent
>   trick: The indepen**dent** voters didn't make a **dent** in the election.

indispensable: absolutely necessary
>   trouble spot: ind**is**pens**a**ble
>   trick: If she **is able**, she's ind**is**pens**able**.

industrial: relating to industry
>   trouble spot: indust**ri**al
>   trick: Watch the **tri**al of the indust**ri**al polluters.

inevitable: unavoidable
>   trouble spot: inevi**ta**ble
>   trick: The collapse of the **table** was inevi**table**.

inflammable: easily set on fire
>   trouble spot: infla**mm**able
>   trick: Trees are more infla**mm**able in su**mm**er.

Trees are more inflammable in summer.

ingenious: clever
> trouble spot: ingen**i**ous
> trick: **I o** (owe) **u** (you) an ingen**iou**s
> explanation.

innocent: not guilty
> trouble spot: in**n**ocent
> trick: **In no cent**ury is murder an
> **innocent** crime.

inoculation: injection
> trouble spot: i**n**oculation (one **n**)
> trick: An **in**oculation is an **in**jection.

insistent: demanding
> trouble spot: insist**e**nt
> trick: Sis was insis**tent** about the **tent**.

instead: in place of
    trouble spot: inst**ea**d
    trick: Drink **tea** inst**ea**d of coffee.

instructor: teacher
    trouble spot: instruct**or**
    trick: The drill instruct**or** gave an
    order.

intellectual: highly intelligent person
    trouble spot: inte**ll**ectual
    trick: You can't **tell** an in**tell**ectual
    anything.

intelligent: smart
    trouble spot: intell**i**gent
    trick: A p**ig** is an intell**ig**ent animal.

interesting: fascinating
    trouble spot: int**e**resting (often
    pronounced "in–tres–ting")
    trick: **Inter**view someone **inter**esting.

interfere: intervene
    trouble spot: interf**ere**
    trick: Don't interf**ere** **here**.

interrupt: break into
    trouble spot: inte**rr**upt
    trick: To **err** is human; so is to
    inte**rr**upt.

irresistible: very attractive
  trouble spot: irresistible
  trick: Your new **lipstick** makes you
  irresistible.

its: possessive pronoun of *it*
  trouble spot: i**ts** (not *it's*)
  trick: The dog f**its its** house.

it's: contraction of *it is*
  trouble spot: it**'s** (not *its*)
  trick: Check **it's** by substituting **it is** to
  see if the sentence still makes sense.

J

jeopardize: put into danger
  trouble spot: j**eo**pardize
  trick: Pronounce *jeopardize* "je–o–par–
  dize."

judgment: decision
  trouble spot: jud**gm**ent (also *judgement*)
  trick: Use your own **judgment,** an **e** or
  not.

K

kerosene: thin oil used as fuel
   trouble spot: ker**ose**ne
   trick: The **oil** in ker**ose**ne has **ene**rgy.

kindergarten: school for young children
   trouble spot: kinderg**art**en
   trick: Teach **art** in kinderg**art**en.

knowledge: information
   trouble spot: knowl**edge**
   trick: Knowl**edge** gives you the **edge**.

L

laid: past tense of *lay*
    trouble spot: l**ai**d
    trick: Did the hen get p**aid** for the egg it
    l**aid**?

language: symbolic communication
    trouble spot: lang**ua**ge
    trick: Pronounce *language* "lan–gu–age."

later: after
    trouble spot: later (one **t**; not *latter*)
    trick: I **ate** la**te**r than you.

latitude: a measure of north and south on the
        globe and earth
    trouble spot: lat**i**tude
    trick: You know you're **at it** if you have
    the right l**ati**tude.

latter: second of two things
    trouble spot: latter (not *later*)
    trick: The l**atter** b**atter** is the be**tter**
    b**atter**.

lawyer: attorney
    trouble spot: lawy**e**r
    trick: **Law ye**s, **lawye**rs no.

league: association
    trouble spot: lea**gue**
    trick: In this lea**gue** it doesn't pay to ar**gue**.

led: guide; past tense of *lead*
    trouble spot: l**e**d (not *lead*)
    trick: I l**e**d him to b**e**d.

leisured: having free time
    trouble spot: l**ei**sured
    trick: N**ei**ther l**ei**sured for**ei**gn counterf**ei**ter could s**ei**ze **ei**ther w**ei**rd h**ei**ght without forf**ei**ting prot**ei**n.

liable: likely
    trouble spot: l**ia**ble
    trick: A l**ia**r is l**ia**ble to cause trouble.

liaison: connection
    trouble spot: l**iai**son
    trick: Pronounce *liaison* "li–a–i–son."

library: place where books are stored and circulated
    trouble spot: lib**r**ary
    trick: No **bra**ts in the lib**ra**ry!

No brats in the library.

license: permission given by law
trouble spot: li**c**e**n**se
trick: They don't **license lice pens.**

lieutenant: officer
trouble spot: li**eu**tenant
trick: Don't **lie u** (you) **lieu**tenant.

lightning: electrical flash in the sky
trouble spot: ligh**tn**ing (no **e** between **t**
and **n**)
trick: Ligh**tn**ing struck the **e** from
ligh**tn**ing.

literature: compositions
trouble spot: lit**era**ture
trick: What's the lit**era**ture of this **era**?

livelihood: means of living
   trouble spot: liv**e**lihood
   trick: To stay al**ive**, you need a
   livelihood.

loneliness: feeling alone
   trouble spot: lon**e**liness
   trick: **One alone** may feel **lone**liness.

loose: not tight
   trouble spot: lo**o**se (not *lose*)
   trick: What would a **loose goose**
   ch**oose**?

lose: misplace
   trouble spot: l**o**se (one **o**; not *loose*)
   trick: It's hard to l**ose** your n**ose**.

losing: misplacing
   trouble spot: l**o**sing (one **o**; no **e**
   between **s** and **i**)
   trick: You'll keep **losing** customers if
   you **sing** at c**losing** time.

luggage: baggage
   trouble spot: lu**gg**age
   trick: **G**et a **g**ood **g**rip on your lu**gg**age.

M

magnificent: wonderful
   trouble spot: magnifi**c**ent
   trick: The **ice** may be magnif**ice**nt, but
   it isn't worth a **cent**.

maintain: keep up
   trouble spot: m**ain**tain
   trick: Even when it r**ain**s and r**ain**s, we
   must m**ain**tain the roads.

maintenance: upkeep
   trouble spot: maint**e**nance (contrast
   with *maintain*)
   trick: Main**ten**ance stops at **ten** P.M.

manageable: controllable
   trouble spot: manag**e**able
   trick: When you're **able** to **manage**
   something, it's **manageable**.

management: administration
   trouble spot: man**age**ment
   trick: This is the **age** of man**age**ment.

mantel: shelf above a fireplace
 trouble spot: mant**el**
 trick: The **elf** sits on the mant**el**.

manufacture: produce
 trouble spot: man**u**facture
 trick: Can we **manu**facture it using **manu**al labor?

marriage: wedlock
 trouble spot: marr**i**age
 trick: **I** must be in my marr**i**age.

marshmallow: kind of confection
 trouble spot: marshm**a**llow
 trick: Marshm**all**ows are **all** sugar.

mathematics: study and use of numbers and
     symbols
 trouble spot: mat**h**ematics
 trick: Teach **them** mat**hem**atics.

maybe: perhaps
 trouble spot: ma**yb**e (often misspelled *mabye*)
 trick: **Maybe** is a compound of **may** and **be**.

meanness: bad temper
 trouble spot: mean**n**ess
 trick: (*Ness*-Enders, page 172)

meant: past tense of *mean*
    trouble spot: me**a**nt
    trick: He **mean**t to be **mean**.

medicine: healing arts
    trouble spot: medi**cine**
    trick: A **medic** practices **medicine** to keep you feeling f**ine**.

medieval: of the middle ages
    trouble spot: med**ieva**l
    trick: Knights **di**ed **vali**antly in me**dieval** times.

menace: threaten
    trouble spot: men**ace**
    trick: The men men**ace** us with their f**ace**s.

mention: refer to
    trouble spot: men**tion**
    trick: Please m**ention** my inven**tion**.

merchandise: goods for sale
    trouble spot: merchand**ise**
    trick: Is it w**ise** to buy used merchand**ise**?

merely: simply
    trouble spot: me**re**ly
    trick: **Me rely** on you, is that **merely** what you want?

The men menace us with their faces.

mileage: distance in miles
    trouble spot: mil**e**age
    trick: There's a full **mile** in **mile**age.

minimum: least amount
    trouble spot: min**i**mum
    trick: We bought the **mini**car for the **mini**mum cost.

miscellaneous: mixed together
    trouble spot: mi**scell**aneous
    trick: **Sc**ience deals with mi**scell**aneous **cell**s.

mischievous: troublesome
    trouble spot: mischie**vo**us (no **i** between **v** and **o**)
    trick: It's grie**vous** to **vou**ch for a mischie**vous** kid.

missile: something thrown or shot
    trouble spot: m**issile**
    trick: A **missile** shouldn't **miss** by a
    m**ile**.

Missouri: U.S. state
    trouble spot: Mi**ssour**i
    trick: We'll always **miss our Missouri**.

misspell: spell incorrectly
    trouble spot: mi**ss**pell
    trick: **Miss Pell** can't spell **misspell**.

moccasins: kind of Indian shoe
    trouble spot: mo**cc**a**s**ins
    trick: Do **c**amp **c**ounselors **sin** in
    mo**ccasin**s?

model: person who shows off clothing
    trouble spot: mod**el**
    trick: I'd love to hear that mo**del** yo**del**
    in the mot**el**.

moisten: make wet
    trouble spot: moisten (silent **t**)
    trick: Mois**ten ten** towels.

monotonous: boring
    trouble spot: m**o**n**o**t**o**n**o**us
    trick: Four **o**'s in m**o**n**o**t**o**n**o**us are
    m**o**n**o**t**o**n**ous** to **us**.

morale: spirit
> trouble spot: mor**ale** (silent **e**; not *moral*)
> trick: Give them **ale** to boost their mor**ale**.

mortgage: pledge of property as security for a loan
> trouble spot: mor**t**gage (silent **t**)
> trick: Pronounce *mortgage* "mort–gage."

mourning: expressing grief
> trouble spot: mo**ur**ning (not *morning*)
> trick: We are m**ourn**ing **our** loss.

movable: capable of changing positions
> trouble spot: mo**v**able (also spelled *moveable*)
> trick: You can move the **e** in or out of **movable**.

municipal: relating to a city
> trouble spot: munici**pal**
> trick: I have a **pal** on the munici**pal** council.

murmur: make low sounds
> trouble spot: m**ur**m**ur**
> trick: "**Mur**der, **mur**der," **murmur**s the crowd.

muscle: type of body tissue
    trouble spot: mus**c**le
    trick: If you have **musc**les, you're
    muscular.

museum: place where artifacts are displayed
    trouble spot: mus**eu**m
    trick: **Use** the mus**eu**m.

mustache: hair on the upper lip
    trouble spot: mus**tache**
    trick: Who said a **mustache must ache**?

mysterious: unknown
    trouble spot: myster**ious**
    trick: **My**, isn't it **my**ster**ious** how **I o**
    (owe) **u** (you) more money?

N

naive: unsophisticated
    trouble spot: n**ai**ve
    trick: M**a, I've** been n**ai**ve.

naturally: as one might expect
    trouble spot: natur**all**y
    trick: Natu**rally**, we're going to the
    rally.

necessary: needed
    trouble spot: ne**cess**ary
    trick: Is **recess necess**ary?

necessity: requirement
    trouble spot: ne**cess**ity
    trick: It's a **pity** that **recess** is a
    ne**cess**ity.

neighbor: person living nearby
    trouble spot: n**ei**ghbor
    trick: Our n**ei**ghbor's **eight** b**ei**ge
    r**ei**ndeer w**ei**ghed too much to send by
    fr**ei**ght.

neither: not either
    trouble spot: n**ei**ther
    trick: N**ei**ther l**ei**sured for**ei**gn
    counterf**ei**ter could s**ei**ze **ei**ther w**ei**rd
    h**ei**ght without forf**ei**ting prot**ei**n.

niece: daughter of one's sibling
    trouble spot: n**ie**ce
    trick: My n**ie**ce gave me a p**ie**ce of p**ie**.

nineteen: ten plus nine
 trouble spot: nin**e**teen
 trick: **Nine teens** *are* **nineteen**.

ninety: ten times nine
 trouble spot: nin**e**ty
 trick: **Nine ty**pewriters typed **ninety**
 times.

ninth: one more than *eighth*
 trouble spot: ni**nt**h (no **e** between **n**
 and **t**)
 trick: The ni**nth** mo**nth** is September.

noticeable: conspicuous
 trouble spot: notic**e**able
 trick: You should be **able** to **notice** the
 e in **noticeable**.

nuisance: bother
 trouble spot: n**ui**sance
 trick: **U** (you) **is** a n**ui**sance.

O

obliged: indebted
   trouble spot: obli**g**ed
   trick: An **oblig**ation makes you feel
   obliged.

oboe: musical instrument
   trouble spot: ob**o**e
   trick: Can you play an ob**oe** with your
   t**oe**?

observant: watchful
   trouble spot: observ**a**nt
   trick: An **observant servant** has kept
   the **ant**s under **observa**tion.

obstacle: barrier
   trouble spot: obsta**cle**
   trick: The obsta**cle** knocked me **cle**ar
   off my bicy**cle**.

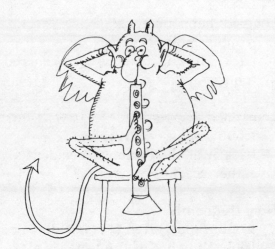

Can you play an oboe with your toe?

occasion: event
     trouble spot: o**cc**asion (one **s**)
     trick: Eat **c**andy and **c**ookies on **s**pecial
     o**cc**a**s**ions.

occasionally: now and then
     trouble spot: occasiona**lly**
     trick: We **all** fail occasion**ally**.

occur: happen
     trouble spot: o**cc**ur (one **r**)
     trick: What might o**cc**ur on a **c**able **c**ar
     ride?

occurred: happened
    trouble spot: o**ccurre**d
    trick: The **c**able **c**ar wreck o**ccurre**d in a hurry.

occurrence: happening
    trouble spot: o**ccurre**nce
    trick: Was the **c**able **c**ar a**cc**ident a **r**ather **re**cent o**ccurre**nce?

often: frequently
    trouble spot: often (**t** is usually silent)
    trick: Nine out **of ten** times is **often** enough.

omitted: left out
    trouble spot: o**m**itted (one **m**)
    trick: The coach o**mitt**ed the **mitt** from our equipment list.

only: alone of its kind
    trouble spot: o**nl**y (sometimes misspelled *olny*)
    trick: I was the **only onl**ooker.

opinion: belief
    trouble spot: o**p**i**n**ion (one **p**; one **n**)
    trick: I wouldn't give a **pin** for your o**pin**ion about **ion**s.

opponent: adversary
trouble spot: op**po**nent
trick: Who wants a hi**ppo** for an
o**ppo**nent in a **tent**?

opportunity: good chance
trouble spot: op**po**rtunity
trick: Be ha**ppy** when an o**ppo**rtunity
ha**ppe**ns.

opposite: as different as possible; across
trouble spot: op**po**site
trick: The hi**ppo** lives on the **site**
o**ppo**site my house.

optimistic: hopeful
trouble spot: opt**i**mistic
trick: **Tim** is always opt**im**istic.

orangutan: type of ape
trouble spot: orang**u**tan (**n** is the last
letter)
trick: Will **u** (you) **tan**, orang**utan?**

outrageous: terrible
trouble spot: outra**ge**ous
trick: This is the **age** of outra**ge**ous
clothes.

overrate: value too highly
trouble spot: ove**rr**ate
trick: It's an **err**or to ove**rr**ate.

overrule: annul
  trouble spot: ove**rr**ule
  trick: It's an **err**or to ove**rr**ule the
  majority.

P

pageant: spectacle
  trouble spot: pag**ea**nt
  trick: Write a **page** about the **ant**
  pageant.

paid: past tense of *pay*
  trouble spot: p**ai**d
  trick: I p**aid** for first **aid**.

pajamas: loose garment worn to bed
  trouble spot: pa**j**amas (one **m**)
  trick: **Pa** and **ma** wear **pa**ja**ma**s.

pale: colorless
  trouble spot: p**al**e (not *pail*)
  trick: A glass of **ale** made my **pal pale**.

pamphlet: small booklet
    trouble spot: pam**ph**let
    trick: **Pam ph**oned for the **pamph**let.

pane: piece or sheet of glass
    trouble spot: p**ane** (not *pain*)
    trick: A **pane** of glass is a **pane**l.

panicky: fearful
    trouble spot: panicky
    trick: Being **sick** makes me pan**ick**y.

parallel: side by side
    trouble spot: para**ll**el
    trick: **All** lines are not par**allel.**

paralysis: inability to function
    trouble spot: paral**y**sis
    trick: **Y** (why) does **sis** have paral**ysis**?

paralyze: take away the ability to move
    trouble spot: paral**y**ze
    trick: **Y** (why) paral**yze** a **ze**bra?

parliament: assembly for making laws
    trouble spot: parl**ia**ment
    trick: **I am** in the parl**iam**ent.

partial: not complete
    trouble spot: partial
    trick: **Part**ial means **part** of something.

passed: past tense of *pass*
    trouble spot: passed (not *past*)
    trick: The **ass** p**ass**ed me by.

past: by
    trouble spot: p**ast** (not *passed*)
    trick: I went p**ast** your house **last** week.

past: former time
    trouble spot: p**ast** (not *passed*)
    trick: **Last** year is in the p**ast**.

pastime: amusement
    trouble spot: pastime (one **s**; one **t**)
    trick: My p**astime**s change **as time** goes
    by.

patience: endurance
    trouble spot: pat**ie**nce
    trick: It takes pat**ie**nce to **tie** a bow**tie**.

pavilion: exhibition area
    trouble spot: pavilion (one **l**)
    trick: The **lion** is in the cat pavi**lion**.

peace: quiet
    trouble spot: p**ea**ce (not *piece*)
    trick: The s**ea** is full of p**ea**ce.

peaceable: not quarrelsome
    trouble spot: peaceable
    trick: **Able** to keep the **peace** mcans
    peaceable.

peculiar: strange
    trouble spot: pecu**liar**
    trick: A **liar** is a pecu**liar** person.

penicillin: antibiotic drug
    trouble spot: penic**ill**in
    trick: When **ill,** take penc**ill**in.

peninsula: land surrounded on three sides by
            water
    trouble spot: pe**n**insula (one **n**)
    trick: I lost my **pen** on the **pen**insula.

performance: doing of a task
    trouble spot: perform**ance**
    trick: The **man** d**anced** a great
    perfor**mance.**

permanent: lasting
    trouble spot: perm**ane**nt
    trick: Is your **mane** perm**ane**nt?

permissible: allowed
    trouble spot: permi**ssi**ble
    trick: Is it per**missi**ble to **miss** Bible
    class?

Is your mane permanent?

perseverant: tenacious
    trouble spot: pers**eve**r**a**nt (no **r** between
    e and **v**)
    trick: The **ant** is **ever** pers**eve**r**a**nt.

persevere: stay with a task
    trouble spot: persev**ere**
    trick: Everyone h**ere** should persev**ere**.

persistent: determined
    trouble spot: persist**ent**
    trick: **Sis** was per**sist**ent about raising
    the **tent**.

personal: private
    trouble spot: person**al** (not *personnel*)
    trick: You're my person**al** p**al**.

personally: in one's own opinion
    trouble spot: person**ally**
    trick: Person**ally**, I like **Sally**.

personnel: people working on a job
    trouble spot: perso**nne**l (not *personal*)
    trick: We have some fu**nny** perso**nnel**
    working in the tu**nnel**.

perspiration: sweat
    trouble spot: perspiration
    trick: When you **perspir**e, you have
    perspiration.

persuade: convince
    trouble spot: pers**ua**de
    trick: Pronounce *persuade* "per–su–ade."

petal: flower part
    trouble spot: pe**t**al (not *pedal* or *peddle*)
    trick: My **pet** snail ate a **pet**al.

physician: doctor
    trouble spot: **phy**sician
    trick: **Y** (why) **ph**one the **phy**sician?

physique: structure of one's body
trouble spot: physi**que**
trick: **Y** (why) **que**stion my physi**que**?

piccolo: musical instrument resembling the flute but smaller
trouble spot: pi**cc**olo
trick: The pi**cc**olo plays from low **c** to high **c**.

picnicking: holding a picnic
trouble spot: picni**ck**ing
trick: Who's the **king** of picnic**king**?

piece: part of something
trouble spot: pi**e**ce (not *peace*)
trick: I want a pi**e**ce of pi**e**.

pigeon: kind of bird
trouble spot: pi**ge**on (no **d** between **i** and **g**)
trick: The **pig** and **pige**on have been here for **e**ons.

pillar: column
trouble spot: pillar
trick: Are there pill**ars** on M**ars**?

pincers: a gripping tool
trouble spot: pin**c**ers
trick: Did you w**ince** when the pr**ince** used pin**ce**rs?

Are there pillars on Mars?

pistil: flower part
  trouble spot: pist**il** (not *pistol*)
  trick: Wait unt**il** the pist**il** w**il**ts.

pistol: small gun
  trouble spot: pist**ol** (not *pistil*)
  trick: I sh**ot** with my pist**ol**.

Pittsburgh: U.S. city in Pennsylvania
  trouble spot: Pittsburg**h** (silent **h**)
  trick: Pittsburg**h** and **H**ershey are both
  in Pennsylvania.

plague: contagious epidemic disease
  trouble spot: plag**ue**
  trick: A plag**ue** of gl**ue** on you!

plaid: pattern of stripes crossing at right an-
gles
    trouble spot: pl**ai**d
    trick: We **laid** out the pl**aid** pattern.

plane: short for airplane
    trouble spot: pl**ane** (not *plain*)
    trick: You need a **plan** to fly a **plan**e.

planned: arranged
    trouble spot: pla**nn**ed
    trick: **Ann** pla**nn**ed.

planning: preparing
    trouble spot: pla**nn**ing
    trick: **Ann** is pla**nn**ing a trip.

playwright: a dramatist
    trouble spot: play**wright**
    trick: The play**wright** **wr**ote **right**-
handed.

pleasant: agreeable
    trouble spot: pl**eas**ant
    trick: The **eas**t coast is pl**eas**ant.

politician: person engaged in politics
    trouble spot: poli**ti**cian
    trick: **Politic**ians must be **polit**e to do
well in **politic**s.

pomegranate: a fruit
    trouble spot: pom**e**granat**e**
    trick: At h**ome** I **ate** a pom**e**granat**e**.

porcelain: kind of ceramic
    trouble spot: porcel**ain**
    trick: The porcel**ain** container has **lain**
    here all night.

porpoise: dolphin
    trouble spot: porp**oise**
    trick: A porp**oise** makes an interesting
    n**oise**.

possess: own
    trouble spot: po**ss**e**ss**
    trick: No one can po**ss**e**ss** the
    Mi**ss**i**ss**ippi.

possible: capable of being done
    trouble spot: po**ss**i**b**le
    trick: It's po**ssible** I'm mi**ss**ing my
    Bi**b**le.

potatoes: kind of vegetable
    trouble spot: pota**toes**
    trick: There were her**oes** facing
    torped**oes** while eating toma**toes** and
    pota**toes**.

Practice driving on ice.

practically: almost
    trouble spot: practic**ally**
    trick: **Sally** practic**ally** broke her neck.

practice: repeated effort
    trouble spot: practi**ce**
    trick: Practi**ce** driving on **ice.**

prairie: a large area of grassland
    trouble spot: pr**air**ie
    trick: There's good **air** on the pr**air**ie.

preceded: go before
    trouble spot: pre**ce**de**d**
    trick: He pre**ce**de**d** me; he **c**ame **e**arlier
    and **d**ied **e**arlier.

preceding: before
    trouble spot: preceding (one **e**)
    trick: **Prece**ding the **rece**ption, pictures
    will be taken.

precious: of great value
    trouble spot: pre**ci**ous
    trick: **I o** (owe) **u** (you) a pre**ciou**s gem.

precocious: advanced
    trouble spot: pre**co**cious
    trick: The pre**co**cious child loves **co**coa.

prefer: favor
    trouble spot: pre**f**er (one **f**)
    trick: I pre**fer** a **fer**n.

prejudice: bias
    trouble spot: pre**j**udice (no **d** between **e**
    and **j**)
    trick: When you **prejud**ge, you have a
    prejudice.

preparation: readiness
    trouble spot: prep**a**ration
    trick: **Pa** taught us prep**a**ration.

prevalent: widely existing or practiced
    trouble spot: preva**l**ent
    trick: **Ale** is the preva**l**ent beverage
    around here.

prey: hunt for food
    trouble spot: pr**ey** (not *pray*)
    trick: A **pre**dator **pre**ys.

principal: head of a school
  trouble spot: princi**pal** (not *principle*)
  trick: The school princi**pal** is your **pal**.

principle: rule
  trouble spot: princip**le** (not *principal*)
  trick: The princip**le** that serves as a
  guideline is a ru**le**.

privilege: advantage
  trouble spot: pri**vile**ge
  trick: It's **vile** that the rich have
  pri**vile**ges.

probably: more likely than not
  trouble spot: pro**bab**ly
  trick: The **bab**y pro**bab**ly did it.

procedure: method
  trouble spot: proc**e**dure (one **e**)
  trick: **Ed** taught me the proc**ed**ure.

proceed: continue
  trouble spot: proc**eed**
  trick: Proc**eed** at full sp**eed**.

prodigy: person with extraordinary ability
  trouble spot: pro**dig**y
  trick: The pro**dig**y **dig**s into books.

professor: college teacher
    trouble spot: profe**ss**or
    trick: Con**fess or** else, pro**fess**or.

prominent: well known
    trouble spot: prom**in**ent
    trick: This pro**min**ent leader is a friend of **mine**.

pronounce: speak aloud
    trouble spot: pron**ou**nce
    trick: Pron**ou**nce the **nou**n.

pronunciation: way of saying words
    trouble spot: pro**nun**ciation
    trick: The **nun** has good pro**nun**ciation.

propaganda: information intended to convince
    trouble spot: prop**a**ganda
    trick: This is **pagan** pro**pagan**da.

propagate: to breed
    trouble spot: prop**a**gate
    trick: **Pa** told us to pro**pa**gate.

propeller: a device with blades used for pro-
pulsion
    trouble spot: propell**er**
    trick: I'm a propell**er** sell**er**.

prophecy: prediction
    trouble spot: prophecy (not *prophesy*)
    trick: Na**cy** made a prophe**cy**.

prophesy: predict
    trouble spot: prophesy (not *prophecy*)
    trick: It takes **s**kill to prophe**s**y.

protein: cellular building material
    trouble spot: prot**ei**n
    trick: N**ei**ther l**ei**sured for**ei**gn
    counterf**ei**ter could s**ei**ze **ei**ther w**ei**rd
    h**ei**ght without forf**ei**ting prot**ei**n.

psychology: science of behavior
    trouble spot: **psy**chology
    trick: **P.S. Y** (why) are you studying
    psychology?

purchase: buy
    trouble spot: p**ur**chase
    trick: P**ur**chase the p**ur**se.

pursue: go after
    trouble spot: p**ur**sue
    trick: P**ur**sue a lost p**ur**se.

Q

---

quantity: an amount
   trouble spot: quan**ti**ty
   trick: There's a large quan**ti**ty of
   garbage in the **ci**ty.

questionnaire: survey form
   trouble spot: questio**nn**aire
   trick: The questio**nn**aire at the **inn**
   raised my **ire**.

quiet: stillness
   trouble spot: qu**ie**t (not *quite*)
   trick: I ate a qu**ie**t d**ie**t of soup and
   bread.

quite: very
   trouble spot: qu**it**e (not *quiet*)
   trick: I took qu**it**e a b**it**e.

R

raccoon: masked mammal
    trouble spot: ra**cc**o**o**n
    trick: A ra**cc**o**o**n is twice the bother (**cc, oo**) of other animals.

ransom: pay money to free a hostage
    trouble spot: ranso**m** (no **e** at the end)
    trick: Ranso**m** To**m**.

rapport: harmony
    trouble spot: rappor**t** (silent **t**)
    trick: Our h**app**y r**apport** needs your su**pport**.

raspberry: kind of fruit
    trouble spot: ras**p**berry (silent **p**)
    trick: I g**rasp** the **rasp**berry.

realize: understand
    trouble spot: r**ea**lize
    trick: **Rea**lity's s**ize** is hard to r**ea**lize.

I grasp the raspberry.

really: truly
 trouble spot: re**ally**
 trick: Are you re**ally** S**ally**?

receipt: proof of purchase
 trouble spot: recei**pt** (silent **p**)
 trick: He's **apt** to forget the **p** in recei**pt**.

receivable: due
 trouble spot: recei**vable** (no **e** between **v**
 and **a**)
 trick: The **valuable**s are recei**vable**.

receive: to get
 trouble spot: rece**ive**
 trick: (*I Before E*, pages 169–170)

recipe: procedure for cooking
    trouble spot: rec**ipe**
    trick: The rec**ipe** says to w**ipe** the r**ipe**
    fruit.

reckless: careless
    trouble spot: **r**eckless (no **w**)
    trick: **R**ick is **r**eckless.

recognize: know someone or something
    trouble spot: rec**og**nize
    trick: Can you rec**og**nize your d**og**?

recommend: suggest
    trouble spot: re**comm**end
    trick: What re**co**rds do you re**comm**end
    for su**mm**er?

recruit: new member
    trouble spot: recr**uit**
    trick: The new recr**uit** wears a s**uit**.

refer: send
    trouble spot: refer (one **f**)
    trick: **Ref**er the quarterback to the **ref**.

referred: mentioned
    trouble spot: ref**err**ed
    trick: He was ref**err**ed in **err**or.

regrettable: unfortunate
   trouble spot: regre**tt**able
   trick: How **regrettable** to **regret table**s.

rehearse: practice
   trouble spot: reh**ear**se
   trick: **Hear** the band reh**ear**se.

reindeer: hooved mammals
   trouble spot: r**ei**ndeer
   trick: Our n**ei**ghbor's **ei**ght b**ei**ge
   r**ei**ndeer w**ei**ghed too much to send by
   fr**ei**ght.

relevant: pertinent
   trouble spot: relev**ant**
   trick: A picnic's relev**ant** to **ant**s.

relief: help
   trouble spot: rel**ie**f
   trick: A **lie** offers no rel**ie**f.

religious: devout
   trouble spot: relig**iou**s
   trick: Do **I o** (owe) **u** (you) a relig**iou**s
   experience?

remembrance: recollection
   trouble spot: remem**br**ance (no **e**
   between **b** and **r**)
   trick: The tree had a remem**br**ance of
   branches past.

rendezvous: place set for a meeting
> trouble spot: rendezvou**s**
> trick: Pronounce *rendezvous* "ren–dez–vous."

renown: great fame
> trouble spot: re**n**ow**n** (no **k**)
> trick: **Now** she has **renow**n in **Reno**.

repentant: sorry
> trouble spot: repent**a**nt
> trick: The **ant** is repent**ant**.

repetition: repeating
> trouble spot: rep**e**tition
> trick: My **pet** loves re**pet**ition.

representative: one who acts or speaks for others
> trouble spot: represent**a**tive
> trick: A **representativ**e gives us **representati**on.

rescind: cancel
> trouble spot: re**sc**ind
> trick: **Resc**ind the **resc**ue call.

response: answer
> trouble spot: respon**s**e
> trick: **S**end a respon**s**e by mail.

restaurant: eating place
    trouble spot: rest**au**rant
    trick: This **restaura**nt has a **res**tful
    aura.

rhapsody: a kind of musical composition
    trouble spot: r**h**apsody (silent **h**)
    trick: That **chap** wrote a r**hap**sody.

rhetorical: relating to the art of using words
            effectively
    trouble spot: r**h**etorical (silent **h**)
    trick: A **rh**eumatic **rh**inoceros practices
    rhetorical **rh**ymes while eating
    rhododendrons and **rh**ubarb in **Rh**ode
    Island.

rheumatic: having pain in joints and muscles
    trouble spot: r**h**eumatic (silent **h**)
    trick: A **rh**eumatic **rh**inoceros practices
    rhetorical **rh**ymes while eating
    rhododendrons and **rh**ubarb in **Rh**ode
    Island.

rhinoceros: large animal
    trouble spot: r**h**inoceros (silent **h**)
    trick: A **rh**eumatic **rh**inoceros practices
    rhetorical **rh**ymes while eating
    rhododendrons and **rh**ubarb in **Rh**ode
    Island.

Rhode Island: U.S. state
> trouble spot: **R**hode Island (silent **h**)
> trick: A **rh**eumatic **rh**inoceros practices **rh**etorical **rh**ymes while eating **rh**ododendrons and **rh**ubarb in **Rh**ode Island.

rhubarb: plant
> trouble spot: **rh**ubarb (silent **h**)
> trick: A **rh**eumatic **rh**inoceros practices **rh**etorical **rh**ymes while eating **rh**ododendrons and **rh**ubarb in **Rh**ode Island.

rhymes: corresponding sounds within paired words
> trouble spot: **rh**ymes (silent **h**)
> trick: A **rh**eumatic **rh**inoceros practices **rh**etorical **rh**ymes while eating **rh**ododendrons and **rh**ubarb in **Rh**ode Island.

ridiculous: absurd
> trouble spot: **ri**diculous
> trick: Get **rid** of that **rid**iculous smile.

role: part in a play
> trouble spot: ro**le** (not *roll*)
> trick: I play the r**ole** of a m**ole** in a h**ole**.

roll: turn
> trouble spot: ro**ll** (not *role*)
> trick: **Roll** the t**roll** off the bridge.

roommate: room sharer
> trouble spot: ro**mm**ate
> trick: I have a su**mm**er roo**mm**ate.

rough: coarse; difficult
> trouble spot: r**ough**
> trick: I th**ough**t I'd b**ough**t en**ough** c**ough** syrup to make it thr**ough** this r**ough**, t**ough** winter.

route: course
> trouble spot: r**ou**te (pronounced like *rout* or *root*)
> trick: I want to take the **oute**r r**oute**.

S

sacrifice: to give up something
> trouble spot: sacr**i**fice
> trick: **If** you sacr**if**ice, I will too.

sacrilegious: violating something sacred
    trouble spot: sac**ri**legious
    trick: You **rile** me with your
    sac**rile**gious attitude.

safety: freedom from danger
    trouble spot: saf**e**ty
    trick: Make something **safe** by working
    on **safe**ty.

salad: vegetable dish
    trouble spot: sa**l**ad (one **l**)
    trick: Give the **lad** a sa**lad**.

salary: payment for employment
    trouble spot: **sal**ary (not *celery*)
    trick: **Sal**ary was once payment in **sal**t.

sandal: kind of slipper
    trouble spot: sand**a**l
    trick: In the **sand Al** wore one **sandal**.

sandwich: bread with filling
    trouble spot: sand**wi**ch (no **t** between **i**
    and **c**)
    trick: **Sand** doesn't make a **sand**w**ich**
    r**ich**.

sapphire: precious stone
    trouble spot: sa**pp**hire
    trick: This sa**pp**hire makes me ha**pp**y.

Salary was once payment in salt.

satellite: orbiting object
    trouble spot: sate**ll**ite
    trick: What does the sate**ll**ite **tell** us?

satisfaction: gratification
    trouble spot: satis**fact**ion
    trick: Satis**fact**ion is a **fact** of life.

satisfactorily: done in an acceptable fashion
    trouble spot: satisfactor**i**ly
    trick: (*Y*-Enders, pages 173–174)

satisfied: pleased
    trouble spot: satis**fied**
    trick: Satis**fied**, he **died**.

scaly: covered with scales
trouble spot: sca**ly** (no **e** between **l** and **y**)
trick: My **scalp** is **scal**y.

scandal: an embarrassing situation
trouble spot: scand**al**
trick: Did you hear about the **panda** sc**andal**?

scarcity: shortage
trouble spot: scar**c**ity
trick: There's a housing scar**city** in this **city**.

scene: portion of film or play
trouble spot: **sc**ene (not *seen*)
trick: Eug**ene** is in a **sc**ary **sc**ene.

scenery: features of landscape
trouble spot: scen**e**ry
trick: The **ene**my hides in the sc**ene**ry.

scent: odor
trouble spot: **sc**ent (not *cent* or *sent*)
trick: Does this new **sc**ent **sc**are you?

schedule: a list of times when certain events
    will occur
    trouble spot: **sch**edule
    trick: The **sch**ed**u**le at **sch**ool is a kind
    of r**u**le.

scheme: plan
    trouble spot: **sch**eme
    trick: You don't need **sch**ool to know
    how to **sch**eme.

scissors: a cutting tool
    trouble spot: s**ciss**ors
    trick: Don't be **sc**ared, M**iss**, by
    s**ciss**ors.

sculptor: artist who creates three-dimen-
    sional works
    trouble spot: sculpt**or** (contrast with
    sculpture)
    trick: I'll be a sculpt**or or** a doct**or**.

sculpture: work of art in three dimensions
    trouble spot: sculp**ture** (contrast with
    sculptor)
    trick: A sculp**ture** is a kind of pic**ture**.

secretary: office worker
    trouble spot: secretary
    trick: A **secret**ary keeps **secret**s.

seize: take
> trouble spot: s**ei**ze (not *cease*)
> trick: N**ei**ther l**ei**sured for**ei**gn counterf**ei**ter could s**ei**ze **ei**ther w**ei**rd h**ei**ght without forf**ei**ting prot**ei**n.

semester: school term
> trouble spot: s**e**m**e**ster
> trick: I'm taking a **sem**inar **se**cond **sem**ester.

senator: member of senate
> trouble spot: senat**or**
> trick: The senat**or** called f**or or**der.

sense: faculty of perception
> trouble spot: sen**s**e (not *cents* or *scents*)
> trick: When you use your **sens**es, you get a **sens**ation.

sensible: reasonable
> trouble spot: sens**i**ble
> trick: You're a sen**sible** **sibl**ing.

separate: move apart
> trouble spot: sep**a**rate
> trick: There's **a rat** in sep**arat**e.

sergeant: noncommissioned officer
> trouble spot: ser**gea**nt
> trick: Pronounce *sergeant* "ser–ge–ant."

serial: story presented in separate parts
    trouble spot: **seri**al (not *cereal*)
    trick: A **seri**al is a **seri**es of stories.

severe: harsh
    trouble spot: sev**ere**
    trick: Are people sev**ere** h**ere?**

shepherd: person who tends sheep
    trouble spot: shep**h**erd (silent **h**)
    trick: A shep**herd herd**s sheep.

sherbet: frozen dessert
    trouble spot: sher**b**et (no **r** between **e**
    and **t**)
    trick: He took **her bet** that he couldn't
    spell **sherbet**.

sheriff: law officer
    trouble spot: sheri**ff** (one **r**)
    trick: A sheri**ff** directs tra**ff**ic.

shriek: make a loud, piercing cry
    trouble spot: shr**iek**
    trick: "Now you d**ie!**" the killer
    shr**iek**ed.

shrivel: wither or shrink
    trouble spot: shriv**el**
    trick: Shriv**el** the **el**f.

Shrivel the elf.

siege: strategic blockade
trouble spot: s**ie**ge
trick: Sold**ie**rs can d**ie** in a s**ie**ge.

similar: having a resemblance
trouble spot: sim**i**lar
trick: These two quarterbacks have
s**i**m**i**lar l**i**m**i**tations.

sincerely: honestly
trouble spot: sinc**e**r**e**ly
trick: **Since** I **rely** on you, I **sincerely**
need you.

skiing: winter sport
trouble spot: sk**ii**ng
trick: Use both **i**'s (eyes) in sk**ii**ng.

snorkel: a device for breathing underwater
trouble spot: snor**kel**
trick: My snor**kel** got caught in the **kel**p.

solder: metal alloy
trouble spot: so**l**der (silent **l**; rhymes with *fodder*)
trick: Who **sold** you this **sold**er?

soldier: military person
trouble spot: sol**di**er
trick: Old sol**di**ers never **di**e.

sole: bottom of foot or shoe
trouble spot: s**ole** (not *soul*)
trick: There's a h**ole** in the s**ole** of your shoe.

sole: one and only
trouble spot: s**ole** (not *soul*)
trick: That's the s**ole** m**ole** in the garden.

sole: kind of fish
trouble spot: s**ole** (not *soul*)
trick: I caught the s**ole** with my fishing p**ole**.

solemn: serious
    trouble spot: solem**n** (silent **n**)
    trick: When you're solem**n**, that's
    solem**n**ity.

somersault: acrobatic stunt
    trouble spot: s**o**mer**s**ault
    trick: **Some somer**s**aults** have f**aults**.

sometime: unspecified time
    trouble spot: **sometime** (one word)
    trick: **Sometime**, like **never**, is one
    word.

source: origin
    trouble spot: s**our**ce
    trick: What is the **sour**ce of this **sour**
    cream?

spacious: large
    trouble spot: spac**iou**s
    trick: **I o** (owe) **u** (you) a spac**iou**s
    place to stay.

specimen: an example or sample
    trouble spot: spe**ci**men
    trick: This **ci**gar is a spe**ci**men.

speech: talk
   trouble spot: sp**ee**ch (contrast with
   speak)
   trick: Exercise your right of fr**ee**
   sp**ee**ch.

sponsor: supporter
   trouble spot: spons**or**
   trick: The spons**or or**dered sh**or**t
   commercials.

squeak: thin, high-pitched sound
   trouble spot: squ**ea**k
   trick: I sp**ea**k with a squ**ea**k.

squeeze: press
   trouble spot: squ**eeze**
   trick: Squ**eeze** the qu**ee**n's **ze**bra.

squirrel: tree-climbing rodent
   trouble spot: squi**rr**el
   trick: The squi**rr**el hu**rr**ies.

stake: pointed stick
   trouble spot: st**ake** (not *steak*)
   trick: Turn this r**ake** handle into a
   st**ake**.

stalactite: underground lime deposit
   trouble spot: stala**c**tite
   trick: Stala**c**tites hang from the **c**eiling.

Squeeze the queen's zebra.

stalagmite: underground lime deposit
   trouble spot: stala**g**mite
   trick: Stala**g**mites grow from the
   ground.

stalk: pursue
   trouble spot: sta**l**k (silent **l**)
   trick: If you don't **talk**, I'll **stalk** you.

stampede: confused mass movement
   trouble spot: stamp**ede**
   trick: The **pede**strian was hurt in the
   stam**pede**.

statement: report
   trouble spot: stat**e**ment
   trick: I h**ate** the st**ate**ment.

stating: expressing
> trouble spot: sta**ti**ng (no **e** between **t** and **i**)
> trick: I'm sta**ti**ng that **tin** is valuable.

stationary: fixed in one place
> trouble spot: station**a**ry (not *stationery*)
> trick: A station**a**ry, unmoving object st**a**nds still.

stationery: paper and envelopes
> trouble spot: station**e**ry (not *stationary*)
> trick: The station**e**ry that you write letters on is pap**e**r.

steak: slice of meat
> trouble spot: st**ea**k (not *stake*)
> trick: You **ea**t a st**ea**k.

steal: take without permission
> trouble spot: st**ea**l (not *steel*)
> trick: When you st**ea**l a m**ea**l of v**ea**l, you're in r**ea**l troubl**e**.

steel: metal alloy
> trouble spot: st**ee**l (not *steal*)
> trick: F**ee**l the st**ee**l wh**ee**l.

strait: narrow waterway
> trouble spot: str**ai**t (not *straight*)
> trick: We caught some b**ai**t in the str**ai**t.

I'm crying while I'm studying.

studying: acquiring knowledge
    trouble spot: stud**y**ing
    trick: I'm cr**ying** while I'm stud**ying**.

subtle: not obvious
    trouble spot: su**b**tle (silent **b**)
    trick: Pronounce *subtle* "sub–tle."

subtly: done in a sly manner
    trouble spot: sub**tly** (no **e** between **l**
    and **y**)
    trick: It was done ap**tly** and sub**tly**.

succulent: juicy
    trouble spot: su**cc**ulent
    trick: The **c**u**c**umber he **lent** us was su**cc**ulent.

suede: tanned leather
    trouble spot: **sue**de
    trick: **Sue** loves **sue**de.

sufficient: enough
    trouble spot: suffic**i**ent
    trick: Is all this stuff suffic**ient** for your cl**ient**?

suffrage: the right to vote; franchise
    trouble spot: suf**fr**age (no **e** between **f** and **r**)
    trick: The fighters for su**ffrage** didn't blu**ff rage**.

suing: seeking justice in court
    trouble spot: su**i**ng (no **e** between **u** and **i**)
    trick: When you're **sui**ng, you're making a **sui**t.

suite: group of connected rooms
    trouble spot: **suit**e (not *sweet*)
    trick: I wore a new **suit** in the wh**it**e **suit**e.

sundae: ice cream covered with syrup
trouble spot: sund**ae** (not *Sunday*)
trick: I **ate** a sund**ae**.

sundries: miscellaneous things
trouble spot: sundr**ies**
trick: The **sun dries** our **sundries**.

superintendent: person in charge
trouble spot: superintend**e**nt
trick: Pay your r**ent** to the
superintend**ent**.

supersede: replace
trouble spot: super**sede**
trick: Super**sede** means to **se**t asi**de**.

superstitious: believing in superstition
trouble spot: super**stit**ious
trick: The super**stit**ious seamstress will
never cross her **stit**ches.

supervisor: person in charge
trouble spot: supervis**or**
trick: A super**visor** wears a **visor** and
gives **or**ders.

supplies: provisions
trouble spot: suppl**ies**
trick: **Lies** are a liar's suppl**ies**.

Urge on the surgeon.

suppress: subdue
    trouble spot: su**pp**ress
    trick: **Supp**ress your urge for **supp**er.

surgeon: doctor who specializes in opera-
            tions
    trouble spot: s**urge**on
    trick: **Urge on** the s**urge**on.

surprise: startle
    trouble spot: surpr**ise**
    trick: Is it w**ise** to surpr**ise** a burglar?

sweat: perspiration
    trouble spot: sw**ea**t (not *sweet*)
    trick: The h**ea**t can make you sw**ea**t.

sweet: relating to one of the four sensations of taste
trouble spot: sw**ee**t (not *sweat* or *suite*)
trick: A b**ee**'s honey is sw**ee**t.

sword: long-bladed weapon
trouble spot: s**w**ord
trick: **Sw**ing a **sw**ord.

syllable: unit of pronunciation
trouble spot: sy**ll**able
trick: **Y** (why) a**ll** the fuss about sy**ll**ables?

symbol: something that stands for something else
trouble spot: symb**o**l (not *cymbal*)
trick: We need a b**ol**d symb**ol**.

sympathy: a sharing of someone else's sorrow or trouble
trouble spot: s**y**mpathy
trick: **Y** (why) should I feel s**y**mpathy for you?

synagogue: a Jewish temple
trouble spot: synagog**ue**
trick: **Y** (why) is the synagog**ue** bl**ue**?

synonym: word with the same meaning as
           another word
    trouble spot: synonym
    trick: **Y** (why), oh **y** (why) does
    synonym have two **y**'s?

T

tail: the rear of something
    trouble spot: t**ail** (not *tale*)
    trick: The t**ail** of the kite will make it
    s**ail**.

tailor: one who makes clothes
    trouble spot: tail**or**
    trick: **Lord**, that tail**or** can sew!

taking: getting possession or use; indulging
           in
    trouble spot: ta**ki**ng (no **e** between **k**
    and **i**)
    trick: The **king** is ta**king** a nap.

tale: story
> trouble spot: t**a**le (not *tail*)
> trick: It takes t**ale**nt to tell a t**ale**.

tambourine: musical instrument
> trouble spot: tamb**our**ine
> trick: **Our** tamb**our**ine so**u**nds fine.

tangible: having actual form
> trouble spot: tang**i**ble
> trick: Are the B**ible**'s truths tang**ible**?

tariff: import tax
> trouble spot: ta**r**iff (one **r**)
> trick: The t**ariff** on t**ar** caused a t**iff**.

tassel: decoration
> trouble spot: tass**el**
> trick: The **el**ephant wore a tass**el**.

tattoo: skin decoration
> trouble spot: t**att**oo
> trick: My c**at, too**, got a t**attoo**.

tea: beverage
> trouble spot: t**ea** (not *tee*)
> trick: I like something to **ea**t with my t**ea**.

technical: relating to applied science
> trouble spot: te**ch**nical
> trick: **Ch**oose a te**ch**nical profession.

My cat, too, got a tattoo.

tee: a holder for a golf ball
    trouble spot: **tee** (not *tea*)
    trick: **See** the golf t**ee**.

televise: to transmit by television
    trouble spot: tele**vise**
    trick: Is it w**ise** to tele**vise**?

temperamental: unpredictable
    trouble spot: temp**era**mental
    trick: This is an **era** of temp**era**mental
    actors.

temporary: not permanent
    trouble spot: temp**o**rary
    trick: This is the **tempo**rary **tempo**.

tenant: person who rents an apartment or a
    house
    trouble spot: te**na**nt (one **n**)
    trick: I have **ten ants** for **tenants**.

tendency: inclination
    trouble spot: tend**e**ncy
    trick: I've a ten**den**cy to hide out in my
    den.

tentacle: armlike appendage
    trouble spot: tent**a**cle
    trick: A tent**a**cle is an **arm**.

terrible: awful
    trouble spot: te**rr**ible
    trick: To **err** is not **terrible**, says the
    Bible.

testimonial: expression of gratitude
    trouble spot: test**i**monial
    trick: **Tim** gave me a te**stim**onial
    banquet.

than: a conjunction
    trouble spot: th**a**n (not *then*)
    trick: I like my **tan** more th**an** your **tan**.

their: possessive pronoun
    trouble spot: th**ei**r (not *there* or *they're*)
    trick: **He** and **I** are th**ei**r sons.

then: at that time
> trouble spot: then (not *than*)
> trick: **When** is t**hen**?

theory: explanation
> trouble spot: th**eo**ry
> trick: **Theo** has a **theo**ry.

there: at or in that place
> trouble spot: th**ere** (not *their* or *they're*)
> trick: You'll find **here** in t**here**.

therefore: so
> trouble spot: theref**ore**
> trick: I'm hungry; theref**ore**, I want m**ore**.

they're: contraction of *they are*
> trouble spot: the**y're** (not *their* or *there*)
> trick: Check **they're** by substituting **they are** to see if the sentence still makes sense.

thief: one who steals
> trouble spot: th**ie**f
> trick: A th**ie**f l**ie**s.

thoroughly: completely
> trouble spot: th**ough**ly
> trick: The Norse god **Thor** was **thor**ough**ly** t**ough**.

thought: past tense of *think*
  trouble spot: thought
  trick: I thought I'd bought enough
  cough syrup to make it through this
  rough, tough winter.

threw: past tense of *throw*
  trouble spot: threw (not *through*)
  trick: I threw the stew.

through: in one side, out the other
  trouble spot: through (not *threw*)
  trick: I thought I'd bought enough
  cough syrup to make it through this
  rough, tough winter.

till: until
  trouble spot: till
  trick: Wait till you get the bill.

to: preposition
  trouble spot: to (not *too* or *two*)
  trick: Go to the store.

tobacco: plant leaves used for smoking
  trouble spot: tobacco (one b)
  trick: Do beer and chocolate chips taste
  as good as tobacco?

together: as a group
  trouble spot: together
  trick: We went together to get her.

tomatoes: kind of fruit
   trouble spot: toma**toes**
   trick: There were her**oes** facing
   torped**oes** while eating toma**toes** and
   pota**toes**.

tomorrow: day after today
   trouble spot: to**m**orrow (one **m**)
   trick: **Tom** will hu**rr**y and do it
   to**m**orrow.

tongue: organ used for taste and speech
   trouble spot: ton**gue**
   trick: Don't put **glue** on your ton**gue**.

too: also
   trouble spot: **too** (not *to* or *two*)
   trick: Did you break your **too**th, **too**?

torpedoes: underwater projectiles
   trouble spot: torped**oes**
   trick: There were her**oes** facing
   torped**oes** while eating toma**toes** and
   pota**toes**.

tough: difficult; strong
   trouble spot: t**ough**
   trick: I th**ough**t I'd b**ough**t en**ough**
   c**ough** syrup to make it thr**ough** this
   r**ough**, t**ough** winter.

Tow the stalled cow.

tow: to pull
    trouble spot: **tow** (not *toe*)
    trick: **Tow** the stalled c**ow**.

toward: in the direction of
    trouble spot: to**war**d
    trick: We're moving to**ward** **war**.

tragedy: disaster
    trouble spot: tra**ge**dy (no **d** between **a**
and **g**)
    trick: This is an **age** of tra**ge**dy.

transferred: moved
    trouble spot: transf**err**ed
    trick: I was transf**err**ed in **err**or.

treacherous: traitorous
    trouble spot: tr**eacher**ous
    trick: The t**eacher** wasn't tr**eacher**ous.

trespass: transgress
   trouble spot: tre**s**pa**ss**
   trick: Tre**s**pa**ss** means tran**s**gre**ss**.

trouble: misfortune
   trouble spot: tr**ou**ble
   trick: **Ou**r tr**ou**bles are **you**r tr**ou**bles.

troupe: a group of actors or singers
   trouble spot: tr**oupe** (silent **e**; not *troop*)
   trick: **Ou**r tr**oupe pe**rforms.

truly: really
   trouble spot: tr**uly** (no **e** between **l**
   and **y**)
   trick: I'll love you tr**uly** in **Ju**ly.

Tuesday: day of the week
   trouble spot: Tuesday
   trick: **T**u**esday** is bl**uesday**.

turkey: fowl
   trouble spot: turk**ey**
   trick: A turk**ey** is the **key** to a
   Thanksgiving dinner.

twelfth: the one after *eleventh*
   trouble spot: twelfth
   trick: The tw**elf**th **elf** was here.

two: number
   trouble spot: **two** (silent **w**; not *to* or *too*)
   trick: There are **two** **tw**ins.

tying: binding
   trouble spot: t**yi**ng (no **e** between **y** and **i**)
   trick: The dog is cr**ying** while I'm t**ying** it up.

tyranny: an oppressive form of government
   trouble spot: ty**ra**n**ny** (contrast with *tyrant*)
   trick: **Y** (why) isn't ty**ra**nny fu**nny**?

U

uncontrollable: not subject to control
   trouble spot: uncontro**ll**able
   trick: This **troll** is uncont**roll**able.

underrate: estimate too low
   trouble spot: unde**rr**ate
   trick: It's an **err**or to unde**rr**ate.

undoubtedly: certainly
  trouble spot: undoub**ted**ly
  trick: **Ted** undoub**ted**ly is the best
  choice.

university: an educational institution
  trouble spot: univer**s**ity
  trick: Scholars **sit** at the univer**s**ity.

unnecessary: not needed
  trouble spot: **unn**ecessary
  trick: (Nay-Sayers, pages 171–172)

until: up to the time of
  trouble spot: unti**l** (one **l**)
  trick: "Un**til** the World **Til**ts," a new
  soap opera.

usage: treatment
  trouble spot: u**s**age (no **e** between **s**
  and **a**)
  trick: The **sage** explained u**sage**.

useful: helpful
  trouble spot: usefu**l** (one **l**)
  trick: One **l** is usefu**l** enough.

using: employing
  trouble spot: u**s**ing (no **e** between **s**
  and **i**)
  trick: **Sing**, u**sing** your best voice.

Ah, Utah!

usually: most often
trouble spot: usu**ally**
trick: **Usually Sally** answers first.

Utah: U.S. state
trouble spot: Ut**ah**
trick: **Ah, Utah!**

V

vaccine: a substance injected into the body in
order to prevent disease
trouble spot: va**cc**ine
trick: How many **cc**'s (**c**ubic
centimeters) of the va**cc**ine do you
need?

vacuum: cleaning machine
trouble spot: va**cuu**m (one **c**)
trick: Pronounce *vacuum* "va–cu–um."

vanilla: a flavoring
trouble spot: vani**ll**a
trick: Van**ill**a makes me **ill**.

various: different
trouble spot: var**iou**s
trick: **I o** (owe) **u** (you) var**iou**s gifts.

vary: change
trouble spot: v**a**ry (not *very*)
trick: M**a**ry won't v**a**ry.

vegetable: plant
    trouble spot: veg**e**table
    trick: We **get** veg**etable**s when we're
    able.

vengeance: revenge
    trouble spot: veng**ea**nce
    trick: Pronounce *vengeance* "ven–ge–
    ance."

veteran: person of long experience
    trouble spot: vete**ran**
    trick: The vete**ran'**s term **ran** out.

veterinarian: animal doctor
    trouble spot: vet**erin**arian
    trick: We took our bird, **Peter, in** to see
    a vet**erin**arian.

vicinity: proximity
    trouble spot: vi**ci**nity
    trick: There's a lot of **vic**e in this
    vicinity.

vicious: evil
    trouble spot: vi**cious**
    trick: As your **vic**tim, **I o** (owe) **u** (you)
    a **vicious** blow.

victim: someone harmed by someone or something
    trouble spot: vic**t**im
    trick: **Tim** is a vic**tim**.

villain: evildoer
    trouble spot: vi**llain**
    trick: The vi**llain** got **ill** in the **rain**.

visible: subject to being seen
    trouble spot: vis**ible**
    trick: Is your s**ibl**ing vis**ible**?

vitamin: organic substance
    trouble spot: vita**min**
    trick: I'll take a vita**min** **in** a **min**ute.

volume: loudness
    trouble spot: vol**ume**
    trick: Is the vol**ume** too high for **u** (you) and **me**?

W

wail: cry
>   trouble spot: w**ail** (not *whale* or *wale*)
>   trick: When you **ail**, w**ail**.

waist: part of the human body
>   trouble spot: w**ai**st (not *waste*)
>   trick: The w**ai**ter has a narrow w**ai**st.

ware: product
>   trouble spot: w**are** (not *wear* or *where*)
>   trick: Put the **war ware**s in the **ware**house.

waste: squander
>   trouble spot: w**aste** (not *waist*)
>   trick: Don't w**aste** the p**aste** in h**aste**.

wealth: riches
>   trouble spot: w**ea**lth
>   trick: W**ea**lth can't h**ea**l you.

wear: have on the body
    trouble spot: w**ea**r (not *ware* or *where*)
    trick: **W**ear an **ear**muff.

weather: condition of the atmosphere
    trouble spot: w**ea**ther (not *whether*)
    trick: **We eat her** food in all **weather**.

Wednesday: day of the week
    trouble spot: We**dnes**day
    trick: Pronounce *Wednesday* "Wed–nes–day."

weigh: to determine the weight or mass of
        something
    trouble spot: w**eigh** (not *way*)
    trick: Our n**eigh**bor's **eigh**t b**eig**e
    r**ei**ndeer w**eigh**ed too much to send by
    fr**eigh**t.

weird: strange
    trouble spot: w**ei**rd
    trick: N**ei**ther l**ei**sured for**eig**n
    counterf**ei**ter could s**ei**ze **ei**ther w**ei**rd
    h**ei**ght without forf**ei**ting prot**ei**n.

welcome: greet
    trouble spot: welcome (one **l**)
    trick: We**l**come the e**l**f.

wharf: dock
    trouble spot: w**harf**
    trick: The w**harf** is at the **har**bor.

where: at what place
    trouble spot: w**here** (not *ware* or *wear*)
    trick: **Where** is **here?**

whether: in case
    trouble spot: w**het**her (not *weather*)
    trick: I don't know **whe**ther or **when** I will come.

which: what ones
    trouble spot: wh**ich** (not *witch*)
    trick: Wh**ich rich** person was it?

whole: entire
    trouble spot: w**hole** (not *hole*)
    trick: **Who** knows the w**hole** story?

wholly: entirely
    trouble spot: who**lly** (no **e** between **l** and **l**; not *holey* or *holy*)
    trick: M**olly** is wh**olly** responsible.

whose: belonging to which person
    trouble spot: who**se** (not *who's*)
    trick: W**hose hose** is it?

wintry: of winter
>trouble spot: win**try** (no **e** between **t**
>and **r**)
>trick: **Try** a win**try** sport.

witch: woman with magical powers
>trouble spot: w**itch** (not *which*)
>trick: A w**itch** can make you **itch**.

wrap: enclose
>trouble spot: **wr**ap (not *rap*)
>trick: After I **wr**ap the package, should
>I **wr**ite the address on it?

wring: squeeze
>trouble spot: **wr**ing (not *ring*)
>trick: **Wr**ing out the **w**ash.

writing: composing
>trouble spot: wri**ti**ng (no **e** between **t**
>and **i**)
>trick: Your wri**ti**ng makes me **ti**ngle.

written: composed
>trouble spot: written
>trick: What's wr**itten** on your m**itten**?

X

xylophone: musical instrument
  trouble spot: **xylophone**
  trick: **X, y** (no **z**) **lo phone** is the way
  you spell **xylophone**.

Y

yacht: pleasure ship
  trouble spot: **y**a**ch**t
  trick: Did **B**a**ch** own a **y**a**ch**t?

yeoman: a petty officer
  trouble spot: **y**e**oman**
  trick: Pronounce *yeoman* "ye–o–man."

Did Bach own a yacht?

yield: to turn over
   trouble spot: y**ie**ld
   trick: **Yie**ld, or d**ie**!

yolk: yellow part of the egg
   trouble spot: yo**lk** (not *yoke*)
   trick: My fo**lks** ate the yo**lks.**

your: possessive pronoun
   trouble spot: **your** (not *you're*)
   trick: **Your** life is not **our** life.

you're: contraction of *you are*
   trouble spot: yo**u're** (not *your*)
   trick: Check **you're** by substituting **you
   are** to see if the sentence still makes
   sense.

Z

zenith: highest point
    trouble spot: **z**enith (not **x**)
    trick: **Z**igzag to the **z**enith of the hill.

zinc: metal
    trouble spot: zin**c**
    trick: Zin**c** can be mixed with **c**opper.

A Dozen Spelling Rules

English spelling is, for the most part, illogical and capriciously crazy. If it weren't, there would be no need for mnemonics.

It's important to note, though, that some regularities do exist. Spelling experts over the ages have propounded scores of rules that aim to clarify the fragile patterns. Many of these rules, alas, are so complex that they defy comprehension or memorization. Others have more exceptions than not.

But a few are serviceable. On the following pages a dozen rules that are the most helpful in combatting demons are presented. One hint in reading the rules: Go slow! Even the most valuable spelling rule looks like spaghetti if you try to speedread it. Take your time. Try to relate the examples to the general statements.

C-Enders

When **c** is the last letter of a word, it is always hard; that is, it is pronounced like a **k.** When adding **-ing, -er,** or **-y** to such words, first insert a **k:**

   panic—panicky
   picnic—picnicking
   traffic—trafficking

The **k** is said to "protect" the hard sound of the **c**. Without the **k**, the **c** might appear to have a soft sound (**s**) as it does in a word like *icing*.

Note that you don't add the **k** when the suffix begins with a consonant. When adding **-ing** to *mimic*, for example, it becomes *mimicking*. But when **-ry** is added, *mimic* becomes *mimicry* (the **k** is not needed to protect the **c** in this case).

Compounders

When spelling a compound word—a word formed from two other words—keep both words whole. Do not drop the last letter of the first word. Do not drop the first letter of the last word. Simply push the two words together.

sidc + walk = sidewalk

This rule holds even when the resulting compound word has a strange-looking double letter in the middle.

book + keeper = bookkeeper
ear + ring = earring
hitch + hiker = hitchhiker
news + stand = newsstand

over + rate = over**r**ate
room + mate = roo**mm**ate
with + hold = wit**hh**old

A classic exception to this rule is *pastime:*

pass + time = pastime (one **s**; one **t**)

You will find a mnemonic for *pastime* in this book.

Contract'ns

Since many contractions have homonyms, mixups are common. Be sure you have the right word: they're/there/their; we're/were. The trick is to expand the contraction to be certain that you have the right word. Suppose you wrote:

I gave the dog *it's* bone.

Try expanding *it's.* You get:

I gave the dog *it is* bone.

The *it is* obviously makes no sense here. Thus, the correct word is *its.*

Remember to put the apostrophe in the right place. The apostrophe goes in the spot where the letters were omitted. Again, expanding the contraction is the test to make. Suppose you wrote *are'nt.* Check it by expansion: *are'nt = are not.* The **o** in *not* is dropped in making this contraction. That means the apostrophe should go between the **n** and the **t**. Hence, the correct spelling is *aren't.*

Double-Enders

When the last two letters of a single-syllable word are a vowel followed by a consonant, double the consonant before adding a suffix.

rip—ri**pp**er, ri**pp**ing

swim—swi**mm**er, swi**mm**ing

top—to**pp**ing, to**pp**ed

The same rule holds for multiple-syllable words when the final syllable is accented.

acquit—acqui**tt**al

control—contro**ll**ing

submit—submi**tt**ing

Note that words like *seat* become *seating* (one **t**) because there are two vowels before the final consonant. Words like *help* become *helping* (one **p**) because they end in two consonants. And words like *benefit* become *benefited* (one **t**) because they are not accented on the final syllable.

E-Enders

Many words end in a silent **e**. Two rules govern what happens to this **e** when you add suffixes.

First rule: Drop the **e** when the suffix begins with a vowel—**-ed, -ing, -ous, -able, -y.**

lose—lo**s**ing
louse—lou**s**y
nerve—ner**vou**s
prove—pro**v**able
tease—tea**s**ing

Important exceptions to this rule are *noticeable* and *courageous*. Also, with many words that end in **ve**, it is permissible to either drop or keep the **e** before **-able**.

love—lo**v**able, lov**e**able
move—mo**v**able, mov**e**able

Second rule: Keep the silent **e** when the suffix begins with a consonant—**-ment, -ful, -ly.**

care—car**e**ful
move—mov**e**ment

Judgment and *acknowledgment* (no **e**) were once exceptions to this rule, but now *judgement* and *acknowledgement* (with the **e**) are accepted. Two more demonic exceptions—*truly* and *ninth*—drop the expected **e**'s. You'll find mnemonics for each of them in this book.

Ful-Enders

Here's a truth that's short and sweet and very power**ful**. Words that end in **-ful** and mean "full of" always conclude **-ful** (one **l**): *helpful, insightful, sorrowful.* There are no exceptions. Isn't that wonder**ful**?

I Before E (and vice versa)

The most famous spelling rule of all is a jingle that goes like this: *I* before *e* except after *c* or when sounded as *a* as in *neighbor* or *weigh.*

I before e	except after c	sounded as a
lie	conceive	reindeer
thief	receive	rein
field	deceive	inveigle
yield	receipt	heinous

There is a problem with this classic truth. There are at least ten exceptions that "prove" this rule; the mnemonic for them is: N**ei**ther l**ei**sured for**ei**gn count**er**f**ei**ter could s**ei**ze **ei**ther w**ei**rd h**ei**ght without forf**ei**ting prot**ei**n.

Ly-Enders

When the suffix **-ly** is added to a word, that root word usually stays the same. Hence:

    clear—**clear**ly
    sincere—**sincere**ly
    slow—**slow**ly
    undoubted—**undoubted**ly

Two well-known exceptions are: *truly* (from *true*) and *wholly* (from *whole)*. You'll find mnemonics for both words in this book.

This (partial) **-ly** truth is especially helpful when facing demons that end in **-lly.**

    conceptual—**conceptual**ly
    hopeful—**hopeful**ly

When you're not sure if a word ends in **-lly,** try to find the root. For example, *practically* comes from *practical*. The **-ly** is simply tacked on the end.

Nay-Sayers

Nearly a dozen prefixes turn root words into their opposites.

able—**un**able
adjust—**mal**adjust
possible—**im**possible
sense—**non**sense

The root never changes when a negative prefix is added. In *misshape* and *unnatural*, the double letters up front may look strange, but the rule holds firm. All you have to know for sure is how the root word begins.

Suppose, for example, you have written *unecessary* (one **n**). Is that correct? You know the word means "not necessary." *Necessary* is the root. To turn it into its antonym, you must add the prefix **un-**. Hence *unnecessary* (two **n**'s) is the right spelling. Ditto for *illegal* ("not legal"), *misspell* ("spell wrongly"), and *immature* ("not mature").

Occasionally, you'll have a bit of trouble figuring out the root. *Innocent*, for example, is based on *in—nocent* (*nocent* being Latin for "harmed"). Usually, though, the roots will be apparent and you'll know to add the prefix.

illegible—il**legible**
irreligious—ir**religious**

The Nay-Sayers' truth should also help you with words like *imagination* (one **m**). This is not a negative form; *agination* is not a word.

Ness-Enders

When adding the suffix **-ness** to a root word, simply add the suffix. The root does not change unless it ends in **y** (happy—happiness). (See *Y*-Enders below.)

close—**close**ness
helpful—**helpful**ness

Remembering that the root does not change will help you defeat mean-looking demons such as:

mean—**mean**ness
sudden—**sudden**ness

O-Enders

Rules about plurals seem to multiply. Luckily, plurals don't cause many problems. Nouns that end in **o**, however, can be demonic. The following observations may help.

If a vowel comes before the final **o**, simply add **s**:

radio—radios

rodeo—rodeos

If a consonant comes before the final **o**, usually add **es**:

hero—heroes

potato—potatoes

However, the plural forms of *mosquito* and *tornado* can go either way—**s** or **es**.

There is one general exception. The plural of most music-related **o**-ending words is formed by adding **s** only.

piano—pianos

solo—solos

Y-Enders

When a word ends in **y**, change the **y** to **i** before adding the suffixes **-ly**, **-ness**, or **-age**. You can slay some of the worst demons using this rule.

busy—business

day—daily

easy—easily

empty—emptiness

jerk—jerkily

lonely—loneliness
penny—penniless
marry—marriage
satisfactory—satisfactorily
temporary—temporarily
There are only a few exceptions, such as:
shy—shyly
sly—slyly
Remember to keep the **y** when adding **-ing**
(even though it may look a little odd).

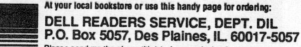